Spirit Messages and Manifestation

The Ultimate Guide to Connecting with Angels and Guides, and Activating Your Quantum Manifesting Power

© Copyright 2026 - All rights reserved.

The contents of this book may not be reproduced, duplicated, or transmitted without direct written permission from the author.

Under no circumstances will any legal responsibility or blame be held against the publisher for any reparation, damages, or monetary loss due to the information herein, either directly or indirectly.

Legal Notice:

You cannot amend, distribute, sell, use, quote, or paraphrase any part or the content within this book without the author's consent.

Disclaimer Notice:

Please note the information contained within this document is for educational and entertainment purposes only. No warranties of any kind are expressed or implied. Readers acknowledge that the author is not engaging in the rendering of legal, financial, medical, or professional advice. Please consult a licensed professional before attempting any techniques outlined in this book.

By reading this document, the reader agrees that under no circumstances is the author responsible for any losses, direct or indirect, which are incurred as a result of the use of the information contained within this document, including, but not limited to, errors, omissions, or inaccuracies.

Your Free Gift
(only available for a limited time)

Thanks for getting this book! If you want to learn more about various spirituality topics, then join Mari Silva's community and get a free guided meditation MP3 for awakening your third eye. This guided meditation mp3 is designed to open and strengthen ones third eye so you can experience a higher state of consciousness. Simply visit the link below the image to get started.

https://spiritualityspot.com/meditation

Or, Scan the QR code!

Table of Contents

PART 1: SPIRIT MESSAGES 1
    INTRODUCTION 3
    CHAPTER 1: UNDERSTANDING GUIDES, ANGELS, AND BEYOND 5
    CHAPTER 2: GETTING STARTED WITH SPIRITUAL AND PSYCHIC PRACTICES 17
    CHAPTER 3: HOW TO CONNECT WITH YOUR SPIRIT GUIDES........... 32
    CHAPTER 4: CONNECTING WITH YOUR ANIMAL GUIDES AND TOTEMS 43
    CHAPTER 5: MESSAGES FROM NATURE SPIRITS 54
    CHAPTER 6: ANGEL SIGNS AND COMMUNICATION 63
    CHAPTER 7: RECONNECTING WITH DEPARTED LOVED ONES AND ANCESTORS.. 73
    CHAPTER 8: COMMUNICATING WITH ASCENDED MASTERS 82
    APPENDIX: SPIRIT MESSAGES – COMMON SIGNS AND SYMBOLS 89
    CONCLUSION 96

PART 2: MANIFESTATION 99
    INTRODUCTION 101
    CHAPTER 1: DECODING MANIFESTATION BASICS............................... 103
    CHAPTER 2: SHAPING YOUR MANIFESTATION MINDSET................... 115
    CHAPTER 3: CREATING YOUR MANIFESTATION TOOLKIT 129
    CHAPTER 4: VISUALIZING THE LIFE YOU WANT 146
    CHAPTER 5: AFFIRMATIONS FOR SCRIPTING A NEW REALITY 157

CHAPTER 6: THE 369 METHOD AND OTHER SECRET
MANIFESTATION FORMULAS 170
CHAPTER 7: QUANTUM JUMPING AND REALITY SHIFTING 181
CHAPTER 8: DAILY MANIFESTATION RITUALS AND ROUTINES 193
CONCLUSION 205
HERE'S ANOTHER BOOK BY MARI SILVA THAT YOU MIGHT LIKE 208
YOUR FREE GIFT (ONLY AVAILABLE FOR A LIMITED TIME) 209
REFERENCES 210
IMAGE SOURCES 227

Part 1: Spirit Messages

Connect with Guardian Angels, Archangels, Spirit Guides, Animal Guides, Nature Spirits, Ancestors, Departed Loved Ones, and More

Introduction

Many people innately feel that certain realms contain an entire world hidden away just beyond the reach of the five senses. Snippets and blimps of that world will sometimes subtly come through, although they will rarely manifest in a physical, observable form. More often than not, the other side will communicate in ways that are noticeable on the inside by those who receive, usually via intuition. More overt messages and even visible symbols from that other realm do materialize, but it's only through higher understanding and practice that you'll be able to truly tune into such frequencies. At that higher level of understanding, you'll realize that messages from beyond aren't as rare as you once thought.

These spiritual messages can carry important insights that can provide guidance, reassurance, comfort, wisdom, or even communication from your departed loved ones. Such signs can be instrumental in helping you surmount life's hurdles, such as grief, uncertainty, and various other challenges. By understanding these signs, you'll be able to strengthen your bond with your ancestors and heritage while also harnessing strength from the elusive realm of spirits, universal energy, and all the unseen forces that keep life churning along.

This book will serve as your comprehensive yet detailed guide, empowering you to detect and interpret these subtle signs from beyond. It will provide you with theoretical knowledge about spiritual messages in all their forms, from the very basics to advanced spiritual and psychic communication. You will also be acquainted with an exhaustive list of signs, messages, and symbols, including their appearance, power, and meaning.

Beyond theory, this book will delve deeply into the practical side of spiritual communication, teaching you about various sources of these messages and techniques that'll help you read into them. You will find that spiritual messages occur in nature all the time and are waiting for you to unlock their meaning through techniques such as meditation, clairvoyance, mindfulness, and plain old intuition. By reading through the following chapters, you'll have become more grounded, spiritual, and reflective. The meditative practices and other techniques you'll become familiar with will also be valuable tools on your overall spiritual journey toward inner peace and balance, propelling you well beyond just the ability to receive spiritual communications.

Rituals, ancient symbols, guardian angels, psychic powers, and nature spirits are only some of the topics that will be covered. The practical exercises you'll learn about will be of interest and use to all spiritually curious individuals, whether they're complete beginners or have already dabbled in esoteric waters. Even though it exists mostly beyond the natural human senses, the hidden spiritual world that you'll dive into through this book harbors valuable lessons and benefits that will undoubtedly translate into your everyday life. Understanding what these messages have to teach can help you resolve emotional and spiritual problems. Still, it can be just as valuable in your other pursuits relating to work, relationships, health, and much more. As you'll soon learn, spirit messages are not entirely different from most kinds of regular, worldly information. *Yet, they require perceptive adjustments on your part if they are to be properly understood.*

Chapter 1: Understanding Guides, Angels, and Beyond

To develop the skills needed to identify and interpret spirit messages, you must first acquaint yourself with a few essential concepts in this area. These are spiritual connections that manifest in people's lives through various means, and they include a range of phenomena that sometimes most closely resemble spiritual entities that dwell in the world beyond. Such forces can be described as spiritual connections because they are the ones that usually come through and act as kinds of intermediaries between living people and other, unseen realms.

Spirits communicate through various forms.[1]

This chapter will provide you with a theoretical foundation to help you understand all the essentials of spiritual communication presented throughout the rest of the book. These include many different sources of spirit messages, including spirit guides, animal guides and totems, angels, and more. Across this book, you will find a mixture of concepts from different cultures, religious practices, and historical periods, all focused on communication with spiritual beings and the realms they inhabit. This opening chapter will also explore the basics of how communication with these forces functions before you can move on to practical steps in the following chapters.

Defining Spiritual Beings

There will be a number of different spiritual beings discussed in this book, which are the usual sources of spirit messages that come through from the other side. They all play different roles and can emit unique messages that carry meanings specific to these spirits and the way they relate to you personally. Needless to say, these spiritual beings aren't something that's readily visible to humans, but they represent interpretations of unseen sources of spirituality and wisdom, as described by various traditions across the world.

Understanding what these beings are and how their messages manifest in your life is essential to learning how to become more in touch with what they have to offer. These spiritual beings will be explored in more depth in their respective chapters later on, at which point you'll be learning about their nature and the practical ways of receiving their messages. The basic overview below will give you a definitive introduction to these concepts, which will also help you determine in advance the spiritual beings most likely to relate to you and your goals in spiritual communication.

Guardian Angels

Guardian angels are a type of spiritual guide that should be a fairly familiar concept in most cultures. Their defining characteristic is their personal relationship with the living person whom they protect and guide in life. According to most traditions, they are assigned, usually at birth, and while they might step back at times, they will be present at least in spirit throughout your life. Guardian angels are your benevolent allies who want you to be on the right path, and there can be more than one at work.

The protective dimension of their role is perhaps their most famous aspect, as guardian angels are believed to do their best to protect people from physical and other harm. Their spiritual messages are usually supportive and reassuring, as the feeling of their presence reinforces the idea that people have someone above who's looking after them. Their love and support are unconditional, even though they might sometimes take a backseat for reasons that are difficult for mortals to comprehend.

Guardian angels also transcend religion and, in various forms, they show up in almost all worldly traditions and orbit around you throughout your life regardless of where you were born. They are subtle spiritual beings that will hardly ever show themselves and will rarely communicate directly. Cryptic messages can come in through numbers or certain objects like feathers, but most of the time, a guardian angel's message will serve the simple purpose of reminding you of their presence. This alone can be a source of great reassurance and security.

Archangels

The main difference between guardian angels and archangels is that the latter are a more universal group of celestial beings. This means that they aren't assigned, and they will rarely have a personal relationship with a person. Instead, their protection and guidance are bestowed upon all human beings. Archangels also have identities that are clearly defined. Some of the most famous ones include Raphael, Michael, Gabriel, Uriel, Chamuel (Samuel), Azrail, and Jophiel. The level of reverence for these and other archangels varies across religions and Christian denominations, with Michael, Gabriel, and Raphael being the most commonly invoked in rituals.

These beings are the direct subordinates of God and, as such, they wield enormous power, with each of them having particular associations and skills, as you'll learn in detail later on. One of the most important strengths of the archangels is their omnipresence and apparent omnipotence, which means that they are able to communicate with many people across the world simultaneously. This accessibility is what makes archangel invocations very popular in all manner of spiritual practices, including communication. When you learn how to understand their signs and messages, archangels will become a source of strength, courage, inner peace, guidance, inspiration, and much more.

Spirit Guides

Serving as an umbrella term, the concept of spirit guides can be taken as referring to each or all of the spiritual beings discussed in this book. One of the later chapters will discuss what that means in more detail, but the main purpose of the term "spirit guide" is to separate those spiritual beings that guide and communicate with people from the many other entities out there. Angelic creatures, animal spirits, departed loved ones, and other beings discussed here are textbook definitions of spirit guides because people can understand them to a much greater extent than paranormal and other phenomena that defy human understanding.

One way to classify spirit guides would be to separate those that show themselves in the physical world and those that do not. Animal guides, for instance, exist in forms that humans can readily observe, unlike angels. There are many forms that spirit guides can assume, with this book focusing on the most well-known and important forms. Beyond classifications, spirit guides are a rather simple concept, as the term simply describes entities, energies, or spirits that exist to assist and provide guidance to living souls. Apart from guides, these spirits are also intermediaries that allow people to feel the touch of things beyond their physical realm. Some spirit guides are constantly present, while others show up at particularly decisive points in your life.

Animal Guides

Animals play at least some role in most religions, but certain traditions give these creatures immense spiritual importance. Concepts like "spirit animals" among numerous indigenous peoples in America or reincarnation in Eastern traditions are prominent examples of the importance of animals in spirituality. Abrahamic religions and their scriptures also abound in animal symbols and anecdotes. Still, the idea of animals being imbued with spiritual essence, at least in the West, can be tied mostly to Native American traditions. For many Native American tribes and nations, animals were given spiritual importance within the larger context of reverence for nature. This includes the firm belief that nature teaches and guides people.

Your spirit animal guide can be any animal that you're particularly attracted to.²

Animal guides can be as diverse as the animal kingdom itself, and, as a larger concept, animal spirit guides are universal in a similar way to archangels. However, different animal spirits carry unique symbolism and meaning, and one person's energy is usually strongly attracted to a specific animal guide. This attraction is felt in the distinct inclination you might feel toward a particular animal, such as an eagle, and how often this animal appears in your dreams. It can also be an animal that you frequently run into, seemingly by chance, while you can't help but feel that there is a reason or meaning behind these encounters. There are many ways to determine which animal is your guide, which will be covered later on in this book.

Nature Spirits

Similarly to animal guides, nature spirits or guides nurture the connection between humans and their natural surroundings. These guides are closely associated with things like healing, energetic purification, grounding, balance, and tranquility. They can also be referred to as elemental spirits. Nature spirits come in various forms, including beings that you can't see, such as fairies or inhabiting aspects of nature that exist in the physical world. The latter includes parts of the world other than animals, such as trees.

Nature spirits also relate to the four basic elements of water, fire, air, and earth. In all forms of spirituality that focus on connecting with nature, the elements are an absolutely essential component of countless rituals.

The importance of the elements cannot be overstated because they make up the entirety of the universe that humans inhabit. The elemental spirit of Earth, for instance, will lend its power to plants while that of water will inhabit the rivers of the world.

Ancestors

Ancestors can be a source of strength even without direct spiritual communication because they often inspire while also eliciting a sense of belonging and continuity that transcends a single person's lifetime. For this and other reasons, ancestors and heritage, in a broader sense, have been the objects of spiritual exploration in virtually all cultures in history in some form or another. This sense of connection that stretches back in time provides meaning and an affirmative existential context for an individual, titillating the fundamental human desire to belong to something greater.

The role of ancestors in terms of spiritual communication can be to guide an individual or an entire community of people. The latter role is the reason why groups of people tend to gather around a shared heritage, acknowledging ancestors as a common thread that binds the community together. Strengthening and exploring your roots can be an immensely empowering pursuit, whether by reading, learning through oral tradition, or any other path. Spiritual communication will only intensify this process and allow you to harness the inspirational power of your ancestry on a much deeper level.

Departed Loved Ones

Departed loved ones are one of the most frequent points of interest for people diving into spiritual communication, especially beginners. The deeply personal bond people feel toward the departed loved ones they knew in life means that these spirits can provide a special kind of guidance and reassurance. Such connections can also be sought as a means of attaining closure and resolving residual emotional issues that you didn't get to address while your loved one was still alive.

Despite some negative connotations attributed to them by popular culture, the spirits of the departed aren't ghosts or malicious paranormal entities whose purpose is to torment the living. On the contrary, connecting with these spirits can provide comfort and important insights essential to improving your life. However, connecting with the departed should not interfere with the natural grieving process. It's about nurturing a spiritual and intuitive connection with someone you care about while processing the fact of their departure in an emotionally healthy manner. As counterintuitive as it might seem, establishing a connection with the departed can help you process grief. There are many other potential benefits to this form of spiritual communication, which only you can know based on your personal needs and your past relationship with the person in question.

What Is Spiritual Communication?

While spiritual communication is an expansive term, like many of the concepts that will be studied in this book, in essence, it's all about how the universe speaks to you. When you consider the universe as a system of different realms that are all intertwined by certain energies, you'll begin to realize that there is a particular language at play that you can learn and understand. It's about realizing that you, as a creature with a degree of your own spirituality and imbued with universal energy and life force, are constantly being guided and influenced by the invisible touch of other energies. In the context of this book, these energies take the form of spiritual beings or guides.

It might be a difficult concept to wrap your head around at first, but it's rather straightforward in essence. One way to look at it is through the concept of prana, which originates in the traditions of Hinduism and related religious practices on the Indian subcontinent. The idea of prana permeates yogic traditions, alternative medicine, martial arts, and some of the biggest religions in the world. You can consider prana to be an invisible energetic thread that intertwines all things in this universe, whether living or inanimate. It flows through you, other beings and objects, and all layers of reality. Because of its omnipresence and interconnectedness, prana is seen as a fundamental force of life that keeps the whole universe churning along.

As such, every person has one physical and one spiritual or energy body. According to Eastern teachings, the energy flowing through you vibrates at a certain frequency and converges at seven important centers in your body. These centers are known as the chakras, arranged vertically in a particular order and stretching from the base of your spine and up to your head. You will learn more about your energy body and chakras in the next chapter, but remember that the sixth chakra (Ajna or the "Third Eye") governs intuition. Located around your forehead, this chakra is all about perception beyond the five senses, especially through intuition, which is why it's such a popular concept among psychics. Because of this, you can consider your sixth chakra to be responsible for spiritual communication.

The vibrating frequency of your energy body is also noteworthy because these vibrations have a significant impact on the attraction or deflection of certain energies when they meet in the universe. Your frequency can affect how much you'll attract or project negativity and positivity, the kinds of people you'll find agreeable, and the kinds of spiritual beings that will be most likely to speak to you.

The Role of Psychic Abilities

In their broadest sense, psychic abilities include an expansive range of extrasensory powers that allow people to exercise some form of sensing beyond the usual range of the human limits of the five senses. These abilities aren't always related to spirituality. They can include supernatural methods of affecting the physical world through powers such as telekinesis or simply perceiving the physical world beyond visual range. There are countless other examples of psychic powers, but the one that relates most closely to spiritual communication is mediumship or any similar ability.

Everyone can try their hand at developing basic psychic abilities and, with enough practice, develop these skills to a certain level.'

A powerful medium or psychic is someone who possesses the skills necessary not just to receive and interpret messages from the realm of spirit but also to contact the other side. While psychic abilities are integral to advanced spiritual communication, not everyone will have such powers, and some people are naturally more predisposed to developing these skills than others. This is why a wide array of spiritual techniques, practices, and rituals are meant to enhance the ability of regular people to detect and understand spirit messages. With that being said, everyone can try their hand at developing basic psychic abilities and, with enough practice, develop these skills to a certain level. Psychic power is a mighty tool that will play a central role in all of your spiritual communication efforts if you choose to hone these abilities.

The "Four Clairs"

You'll learn more about the "four clairs" through the rest of this book, but the basic principle relates to the kinds of psychic abilities that are all about powerful intuition. All human beings possess at least a moderate level of intuition, and some are undoubtedly gifted in this regard. However, your intuition is a lot like the capabilities of your physical body, which means that it can be improved and strengthened through exercise. One way of doing this is to be mindful of and understand the four clairs. As per established practice, the four clairs include the following:

1. **Clairaudience,** usually described as hearing voices, refers to your ability to receive internally audible messages. Of course, clairaudience is vastly different from hearing voices as a consequence of mental health issues. These inner voices that transmit messages via clairaudience are characterized by calmness and familiarity, never causing discomfort.

2. **Clairvoyance** works similarly to clairaudience, except that it refers to visual messages instead of vocal ones, which usually come in the form of images. These messages can be specific images, scenes, or landscapes, and they are usually metaphorical in the sense that they serve as pointers toward a meaning that you will decipher.

3. **Clairsentience** is about recognizing feelings and what they mean. Feelings are an essential medium of spiritual communication, so there is always a lot to unpack in the things you feel. This is the most common of the clairs by far since virtually everyone is born with some ability to feel emotions or internal sensations, even in their most basic form. Deciphering the messages that come in through feelings requires introspection, which is one of the pillars of strong intuition.

4. **Claircognizance** can be summarized as knowing. In a way, this clair refers to the information you can gather from your intuition, interpreting that information and drawing valuable, rational conclusions from it.

As you can see, the four clairs all feed into each other in some way and come together into one whole. That one whole is your intuition, and the four clairs are just one of the ways in which professional psychics and spiritualists categorize and systematize the practice of intuition. Each of the clairs can be improved and developed individually or along the other clairs, which you'll learn about in the next chapter.

Myths and Misconceptions

Across popular culture, urban legends, and media, there is an abundance of misconceptions and myths surrounding communication with spiritual realms. Due to various ghost stories and legends popularized through things like horror movies, spirit communication is often wrongly conflated with the paranormal, especially in a negative sense. The spiritual beings discussed in this book should not be seen as ghostly caricatures that haunt the realm of the living for nefarious purposes.

Communicating with spiritual beings is about tuning into an invisible realm that exists on its own plane of reality and learning to decipher the few signs and messages that come through. Intuition plays a major role in this communication, and your expectation should not be to conjure up ghosts or any other phenomenon traditionally considered paranormal. Instead of summoning entities for personal gain or any other reason, you'll learn to observe, listen, and understand. While these spiritual beings will hardly appear to you in a physical sense, your skills in spiritual messaging will allow you to intuitively feel their presence.

Spiritual communication is still an undertaking that should be taken seriously and never underestimated or conflated with simple entertainment. This isn't because spirit messages pose any kind of danger. The practices associated with it don't always have to be *too* serious, but spirit messages should be respected because they can carry tremendous meaning and value. The messages that you receive from the spiritual realm will seldom be frivolous or pointless as long as you learn how to fully comprehend them.

Another common misconception is that attempts to receive spiritual messages are dangerous and invite trouble. These fears stem largely from media and popular ghost stories, especially concerning spiritual communication, as approached in this book. Paranormal activity, whether sought or uninvited, has been known to cause discomfort and other problems for people from time to time, which is why it's important to distinguish the spiritual from the paranormal.

Other popular misconceptions state that spirit messages can only be received by using special tools such as Ouija boards. As you'll learn later on, communicating with particular spiritual beings can benefit immensely from things like altars and other props that can enhance your efforts, especially in rituals. However, the Ouija board is more associated with the paranormal and relates closely to communicating with the dead, which is just one aspect of spiritual communication. It also doesn't rely on intuition, meditation, or most spiritual rituals that will be covered in this book. Ouija boards started as a game and were marketed as such until popular culture and occult spiritualists in the United States gave them a whole new meaning. Intuition, meditation, and psychic abilities are much older and more established methods of contacting the spirit world, and Ouija boards are far from being a necessary part of the process.

Many people also equate spirit guides strictly with concepts like guardian angels, which needlessly narrows down the concept. It's the perception of each person having only a singular guide that watches over them and provides guidance. In reality, spirit messages come from many sources and can be found throughout the world, pointing to a much broader system of energies and unseen forces that work together or separately to provide a whole range of messages. While it would be a simplification of the concept, it would be fairly accurate to see spirit guides as a team of unseen forces, some of which might stick with you personally while others will come and go throughout your life.

Similarly, some people falsely see spiritual communication as a highly esoteric and exclusive practice that only a gifted few can unlock. In truth, you don't really need any special abilities to receive such messages, especially on a simpler level. More than special esoteric abilities, spirit messaging is primarily about knowledge and your ability to listen on a deeply intuitive level.

Being contacted by the other side also doesn't necessarily require you to enter some kind of special mental state, such as deep meditation. Spirit messages can and will come to you in your normal, wakeful state, even though meditation plays a major role in honing your ability to hear, see, and understand more of what you're receiving. The messages will also come in your dreams, or they can come in when you're out and about, running chores or working. There are very few rules on when, where, and how a spirit message might arrive. The only rule is that you must know what to look for and how to read it.

Furthermore, it's important to understand that being in contact with any kind of spiritual guide is not about relinquishing control of your life. These beings aren't there to overtly intervene in your life and make your decisions for you. Their messages and wisdom are subtle signs that can help you make the right call, choose your direction, or simply feel more peaceful and balanced. At most, spiritual messages will gently nudge you in the right direction, but you will always have to remain at the steering wheel.

Overall, it's important to manage your expectations and also put your mind at ease. Spiritual communication will not immediately solve your problems, but it also won't summon a frightening ghostly entity to terrorize you or anyone else. Like meditation or standard religious practice, communicating with spirits is primarily about finding peace within yourself, becoming more grounded, and firmly interlocking your own spirit with the greater cosmic interplay of energy and spirits. Whether you want a more personal spiritual connection with someone who passed away or the universe itself, there is nothing paranormal or dangerous about these practices. There is also no obstacle to any beginner who might want to use these teachings to live a more spiritual existence.

Chapter 2: Getting Started with Spiritual and Psychic Practices

Before you delve into the practical methods of reading spiritual messages, it's important to understand the value of laying down a strong spiritual foundation. The best way to do this is to learn about your energy and how you can develop your spirituality in a broader sense that relates to more than just spirit messages. This entails learning about basic spiritual practices like meditation, breathing exercises, and visualization. It also means strengthening your intuition by developing the four clairs.

You must be in tune with your own spirituality to be more versed in the spiritual realm.'

You don't have to be a spiritual guru to read spiritual signs and messages, especially if you use the techniques that will be discussed in subsequent chapters, but spiritual work can only enhance the process. The more harmonious your energy and the more spiritually balanced you are, the more the spiritual realm will be unlocked to you. This chapter will provide you with an introduction to general spiritual work, elaborate on the four clairs of intuition, and provide you with a few exercises that you can adopt into your daily routine. Spiritual work like meditation has a plethora of well-known benefits to mental, emotional, and physical health that will be a welcome addition to your life regardless of your efforts to communicate with the spirit world.

The Importance of Spiritual Foundations

For about as long as human beings have been able to think, they've been expressing interest in the spiritual side of their lives. Countless cultures and civilizations have all contributed their customs, interpretations, and traditions to the larger human effort to explore spirituality. As such, spiritual work is an incredibly broad term that can entail any number of practices that you find most agreeable. The native religion that's prevalent in your place of birth certainly offers many avenues toward the exploration of your spirituality, but in the age of information, you can learn about and incorporate many other traditions and teachings to enhance your spiritual life.

There are a few foundational spiritual skills that are worth mentioning, which you are encouraged to explore in much more depth. Apart from developing the four clairs, it's a good idea to explore various forms of meditation while also learning about the power and importance of visualization. Both of these concepts play prominent roles in some of the foreign practices that have recently gained a lot of traction in the West, such as yoga. Furthermore, spiritual protection and psychic defense are also worth studying to strengthen your spiritual foundations even further.

In terms of meditation, it's up to you to decide how deep you want to dive into its techniques. Meditation is a very broad term that includes anything from basic and beginner-friendly mindfulness exercises to advanced yogic practices that involve tremendous effort and knowledge. Fortunately, there are many ways to approach meditation, at least in its basic form, without being a yogic master or studying Eastern traditions in depth. A couple of simple exercises that will soon be discussed will help you in that regard. The main benefit of meditation, particularly with regard to spiritual communication, is that it will make you more present and aware. On top of that, it strengthens and cleanses your energy, reducing interference from unwanted sources and making spiritual messages clearer.

Similarly, visualization is another concept that's simple in principle yet instrumental in all manner of spiritual practice, especially when it comes to communication. Visualization is a powerful exercise in mental strength, usually incorporated into meditation and various rituals. One of the key goals of visualization is to create, shape, direct, and otherwise modify the energies that pass through you or originate within you. It has a lot to do with the power of intention and focus to manifest certain intentions from your mind into the real world.

Overall, there are many ways to purify yourself spiritually and strengthen your energy, and the best approach is to adopt a routine that best suits your goals and lifestyle. You can do this by strengthening and fortifying your energy or simply by achieving a higher degree of balance and inner peace. Regarding spiritual communication, your goal should be to reduce any factors of stress that negatively affect your energy to minimize interference. In the process, you'll sharpen your intuition, increase awareness, and establish a firm energy base for more sensitive work, such as spiritual communication.

The Energy Body

There are many ways in which spiritual practitioners have tried to explain concepts such as universal and personal energy over the centuries. One of these interpretations concerns something called the energy body, which is one of the foundational concepts in all sorts of esoteric, meditative, yogic, and other practices. Your personal energy can also be interpreted through the well-known concept known as the aura.

Being an expert on what your energy body is won't be a fundamental prerequisite for reading spiritual messages, but it will go a long way toward helping you lead a more spiritual life. The tips and exercises that will be discussed later in this chapter will be much easier to understand if you first get a basic idea of how your personal energy works, what it is, and what components it features.

If universal energy can be described through concepts such as prana, then the energy body represents you as a concentration of energy that exists and vibrates at a certain frequency. This vibration, susceptible to positive and negative changes, works as your personal energetic signature. It determines how you and your personal energy interact with the universe and many other forms of energy you'll come into contact with during your life. These include the energy of other people, objects, spaces, creatures, or pulses from other realms.

There are a few different interpretations as to how your energy body can be broken down and defined, although they all describe the same thing and usually involve some description of a system of various parts. For instance, you can see your energy body as having five layers, which are known as the "subtle bodies." The five subtle bodies of your energy each refer to a certain domain or aspect of your energy, including your physical and etheric bodies, emotions, mentality, and spirituality. One of the main goals of energy work and spiritual exercises is maintaining a fine balance among these layers and having them work as a harmonic whole. When in balance, the layers come together into a strong and healthy energy field around you, which can also be called your aura.

The chakra system is similar to the idea of the subtle bodies or layers in that it also places great emphasis on balance and harmony. Since the seven chakras are defined as energy nodes or points where your energy converges, they can also be seen as important channels of communication between your physical and energy bodies. As both prana and your own energy need to flow smoothly and continuously through the chakras, spiritual practices such as yoga and meditation attribute great importance to unblocking the chakras and keeping them clear.

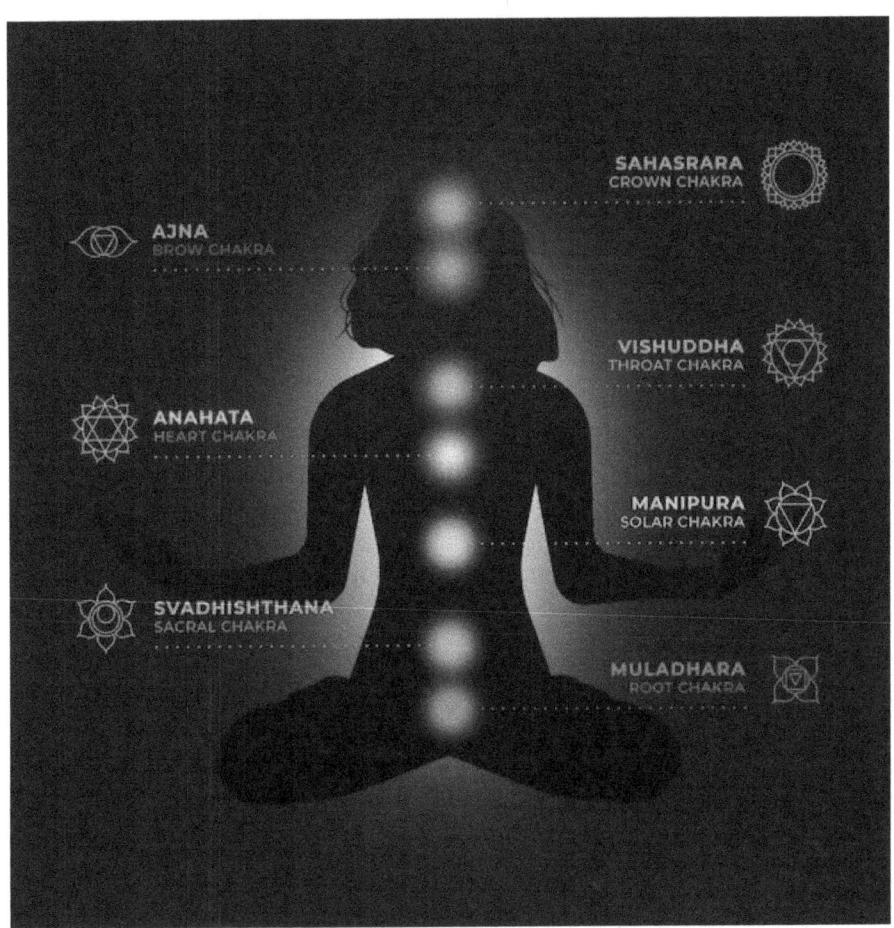

The chakras.[5]

Keeping your sixth chakra (Ajna) clear is especially important for spiritual communication because of its strong association with intuition. This so-called Third Eye is what will allow you to see and intuitively derive meaning from spirit messages. For this reason, there will be a number of exercises throughout the remainder of this book that will focus on either strengthening your Ajna or using its power to enhance rituals and see the messages from spirit guides with more clarity.

Practical Spiritual Exercises

The following tips and exercises are all about strengthening your spiritual foundations and getting acquainted with basic spiritual skills. Developing these skills will help harmonize your energy and improve your overall well-being in your daily life, so they represent a broader set of skills that don't relate solely to spiritual communication. Some of these practices can also play direct roles in rituals and exercises that relate specifically to receiving and decoding certain kinds of spiritual messages.

Breath Awareness

Breath awareness or mindful breathing is a staple of meditation and yoga, especially pranayama yoga, which is built around "breathwork." This is because, in yogic tradition, the function of breathing is seen as the most basic way of channeling the energy of prana through one's body. This means that altering your breathing in certain ways or paying attention to it for the purposes of meditation can significantly affect your energy.

In practical terms, breath awareness works well as an overture to any spiritual exercise or ritual because it's a way for you to enter a state of relaxation. Basic breath awareness is as simple as it sounds since it just entails an intense focus on your breathing process. It's the simplest form of mindfulness, which aims to drown out background noise and distractions while making you completely present, attentive, and relaxed. This can work with any object under meditative focus, but breathing is the simplest method.

Simply find a peaceful and quiet place and make sure that you are as comfortable as possible by wearing loose, soft clothes and taking a simple meditative position. You can sit normally in a comfortable chair or on a soft cushion on the ground, where you can cross your legs, straighten your back, and let your hands rest on your thighs or knees. Begin by shifting your attention to your breathing without trying to breathe manually or automatically. How you breathe is not important. The goal is to become aware of your breathing without reading too much into it or trying to alter it in any way.

Make yourself the observer and focus on how air moves through your nostrils or how your lungs inhale and exhale. Stay focused until nothing except your breathing occupies your attention. You might find this to be more difficult than expected, but if you maintain such focus for long enough, you'll enter a state of basic mindfulness, and mental clutter will fade from your mind. With enough practice, you'll be able to practice mindful breathing without hiding away in a quiet place, allowing you to enter a state of relaxation when you're doing chores or running errands.

Grounding Meditation

Grounding is another simple form of beginner-friendly meditation, and it's focused on strengthening and nurturing your bond with nature and its energy. It's about figuratively rooting yourself via focused energy in the earth, which promotes feelings of harmony, stability, and mental clarity. You can ground yourself in various ways and places, but natural settings are clearly the best choice. Grounding is meditative, but it's not a specific exercise with rigid instructions. Although it's meditative in nature, it doesn't always have to entail an actual meditation ritual.

Meditating in a forest or by a lake naturally entails grounding, but grounding also occurs through a number of other outdoor activities. Taking a long, lonesome walk in the woods while engaging in some basic mindfulness can be a grounding ritual. Essentially, you can create whatever routine or exercise corresponds to your personal preferences, and it will constitute grounding as long as it makes you feel closer to nature and relaxes your mind and spirit. The goal is to be at peace and develop a clear awareness of belonging in the natural world. In that sense, you can ground yourself at the park or even at home and enhance this feeling through simple adjustments like walking barefoot.

Energy Alignment

Aligning your energy means attaining balance and harmony within yourself, which can be achieved by any number of means. The preferred method will depend on the kind of problem that's causing instability in your energy, such as blocked chakras, negative energy attachment, and many other issues. Affirmations, visualization exercises, gratitude rituals, regular yoga, and meditation are only some of the methods applicable to energy alignment.

Beyond spiritual exercises, it's important not to neglect your physical health. A healthy body is home to a healthy spirit, which means that the state of your energy has a lot to do with how you're doing physically. It's no accident that many traditions in Eastern alternative medicine treat physical and spiritual health as inseparable, such as by approaching health issues through the chakra system. The process works both ways, so if you're feeling spiritually unstable or energetically diminished, it could be a simple matter of introducing healthy routines and habits into your life. This means regular exercise, outdoor activities, and especially dietary adjustments.

Third Eye Meditation

Meditating with a focus on your Third Eye is simply about growing your awareness of the sixth chakra and focusing your energy on it. The goal is to clear and strengthen the Ajna so that it enjoys a free and uninterrupted flow of energy that will allow it to function at peak capacity. Such meditation is aimed at empowering your intuition via your Third Eye chakra, which can be done in a number of ways. Keep in mind that meditating on your sixth chakra doesn't necessarily mean "activating" the Third Eye.

A simple meditation to rejuvenate the Third Eye starts with a certain intention, such as cleansing the sixth chakra or infusing it with fresh energy to prepare it for the intuitive aspects of spiritual communication. After that, assume your most comfortable meditative position and make sure to keep your back straight. The meditation should begin with a yogic breathing exercise meant to alternate between relaxing and tensing your body.

Breathing exercises strengthen your third eye.⁶

Inhale a deep breath and hold it while tensing the muscles across your body and counting to six. At the six-second mark, exhale the air in two parts with a tiny pause in between, making sure that the first exhale is shorter than the second. As you carry out this double exhale, relax all the muscles in your body. This process should be repeated three times, and remember to keep your intention in mind. This breathing exercise is a meditation in itself, but it can also be just an introductory part of a more complex meditation.

You can complement this exercise with something called the "expanding the gaps exercise." As usual, take a comfortable meditative position and straighten your spine, once again focusing on your breathing. The exercise is similar to basic breathwork in that you'll just be observing your natural breathing pattern, with the addition of a simple mantra like Om. The key difference is that your focus will not rest on the breathing itself but on the short intervals right between exhaling and inhaling. Stay still and simply observe the gap as it naturally occurs without trying to create or extend the gaps.

After these stages, you can move on to basic visualization focused on your Third Eye. With your eyes closed, try to internally look upward toward your sixth chakra without too much tension in your eyeballs, focusing on the mental image of your Ajna as it pulsates above your eyebrows. You should stay focused on the Third Eye and visualize peaceful energy flowing through it, spending up to ten minutes in a state of meditative breathing and relaxation as you utilize your mantra.

White Light Visualization

This visualization or meditative exercise focuses on visualizing and using something called white light. A common visualization technique, white light is used for spiritual defense, cleansing rituals, fighting negative energies, and much more. It's a concept with a wide application that you can incorporate into many rituals because of its simplicity in principle, with the point of creating and directing energy toward a particular goal.

For example, white light can be visualized to create a protective energetic layer that will have cleansing and fortifying effects on your energy. While this exercise requires powerful visualization, the ritual itself can be quite simple. All you have to do is enter a meditative state and begin visualizing a powerful white light by using real-world examples as a reference. Conjure up a mental image of things like snowy landscapes on a sunny day or sunlight dancing on water. Make it your intention to absorb this light as a protective force whose power will be used to make your energy stronger.

Picture the enveloping glow of this white light descending upon you from above and concentrating all around you. While continuing your meditation, try to visualize the white light and the air around you morphing into one field of energy. Use your breathing to inhale this energy and focus on the sensation of the air entering your lungs and diffusing throughout your body, visualizing the energy of white light entering every fiber of your body and spirit. Visualize your energy body and how it feeds on the white light that you're absorbing, becoming more radiant and stable in the process.

Sacred Space Visualization

This is a visualization exercise because it's all about creating a figurative space within your mind. This mental place is where you can go when trying to communicate with your spirit guides or engage in any other spiritual practice, especially meditation. Even though you'll be creating a mental sanctuary, it's still necessary to find a calm physical retreat for such exercises, too, such as a tranquil garden or a particularly comfortable and quiet place in your home. It doesn't matter where the place is as long as it inspires feelings of safety and calm.

To create a sacred mental space, you only need to position yourself comfortably and eliminate all distractions, especially electronic devices. As always, focus on your breath as you close your eyes and begin visualizing the air you breathe as a torrent of rejuvenating energy that fills every fiber of your being, both spiritually and physically. As you exhale, visualize the breath carrying all tension and stress outward, removing it from your body. Banish everything but the present moment from your mind, and picture yourself occupying a place tucked away in the deep recesses of your mind where no outside interference can touch you.

Picture this as a place where nobody but you and your spirit guide can enter, seeing it as a retreat where you'll come back whenever you need to. It's an escape where you and your spirit guides can bond and where you come for their guidance. Assure yourself fully that the entire universe has guided you to this place and moment so that you can unveil the world that exists beyond your senses, all with the goal of meeting your spirit guide. It can take a lot of practice to develop your visualization skills to such a level, but after some persistent repetition, you'll start to feel detachment from worldly affairs and problems or even your physical surroundings. This is when you'll know it's working, and your withdrawal into this sacred mental space will become a powerful tool to guide yourself into meditation, as you'll soon learn.

Third Eye Activation

Imbuing your Third Eye with peaceful energy and cleansing its chakra, if practiced long enough, will put you in a position where you might be able to figuratively activate your Third Eye. This is best done via various visualization exercises, which can be incorporated into your other meditation exercises or practiced on their own. The purple lotus visualization, for instance, is a common exercise with the potential to greatly stimulate your Third Eye.

The purple lotus is a simple visualization that relies on powerful symbolism. All you have to do is close your eyes during meditation and place your focus on the Third Eye as you would in previously discussed exercises. Once you're aware of the chakra and its location in your head, gradually shift your focus toward visualizing the image of a purple lotus flower emerging right where your Ajna is. Picture it as an opening flower featuring eight petals, representing your Third Eye and the action of opening it. Focus intensely on this image for at least a few minutes until you can vividly observe the image in your mind.

You can also use colors to visualize the activation of your Third Eye by imagining a simple dot in the middle of your visual field. Visualize it as a purple dot to potentiate its energy by using the color related to the Ajna. Visualizing this dot with your eyes open represents a more advanced level of this exercise, so you could begin with your eyes closed and slowly work your way up to the level where you can visualize at all times. Once you master visualizing the purple dot, you can try conjuring up more complex shapes in your vision. This kind of visualization is all about practice, and the more you do it, the stronger your visualization and intuition skills will become.

Developing the Four Clairs

As briefly mentioned earlier, your intuition, along with the four clairs, is something that you can develop on your own. Approaching intuition development through the four clairs allows you to categorize the work required into four separate chunks because each clair is associated with one aspect of your intuition. This makes it easier to build your intuition from the ground up and ensure that each component is as strong as the rest, giving them equal effort and attention.

1. Clairvoyance – Clear Seeing

Since clairvoyance is all about "seeing" with your intuition, it's naturally associated with the Third Eye or Ajna. Any exercise or meditation that you engage in with the goal of strengthening or activating your Third Eye will strengthen your clairvoyant abilities. You should treat your intuition just as you would a muscle, which means that the more you exercise it, the stronger it will get.

It's important to understand that, among humans, the ability to visualize is a spectrum. Some people have a natural gift of powerful visualization while others struggle to form images in their minds, but everyone can try to practice their visualization for some improvement.

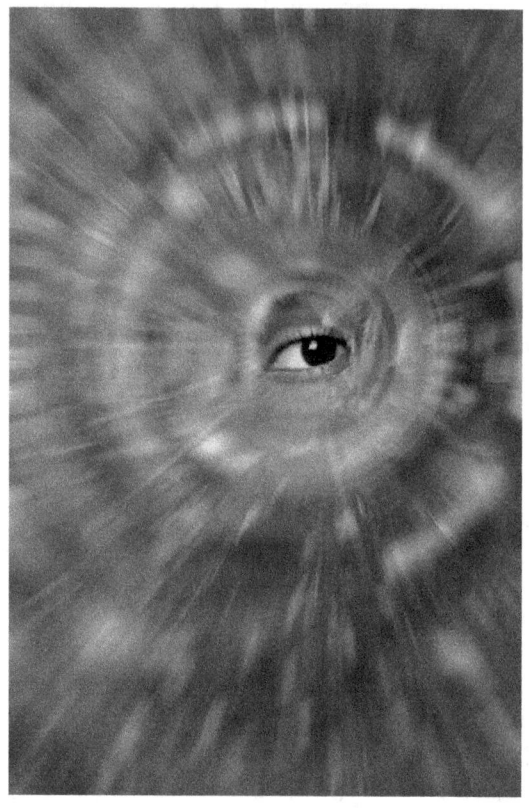

Clairvoyance is all about "seeing" with your intuition.⁷

Beyond meditation revolving around your Third Eye, any visualization will function as a workout routine for your clairvoyance. A simple way to determine the power of your visualization is to observe the things happening in your mind when someone speaks to you. The information you receive from someone else should form certain images in your mind, and if it doesn't, you should make a conscious effort to form them. In the absence of aphantasia, which is the inability to visualize, your visualization skills will get stronger the more you try and create mental images to portray outside information.

You can also form an exercise routine at home to strengthen your visualization and enhance your clairvoyance in the process. Take an inanimate object of your choice and place it somewhere in front of you, placing it in a way that ensures it won't move. Face the object, sit down, relax yourself, and focus intently on that object. Breathe smoothly and intensify your focus on the object as you gradually become aware of your periphery as well, but remain focused on the object.

While still looking at the main object, shift only your thoughts to the objects in your peripheral vision and all around you. No matter what you think you're seeing in your periphery, keep your eyes on the central object and only let your thoughts wander. Remain in this state for up to five minutes, and then write down everything you saw and how it made you feel. On paper, this is a simple exercise, but it will promote a stronger bond between the visual and the mental. After a period of repetition, you might notice that, in general, the images in your mind are becoming more detailed. You can try doing the same exercise in a setting you're less familiar with since you're likely to know your home very well, leaving very little room for imagination.

2. Clairaudience – Clear Hearing

While clairaudience is about "hearing" information within your mind, it's still profoundly connected to your physical sense of hearing. Apart from deafness, there is no sound-related version of a disorder like aphantasia. A healthy mind can still operate even if its ability to visualize is impaired or non-existent, but there is no disorder where you'll be able to hear selectively. Hearing can be diminished for some people, but they'll still experience a range of sounds if it's loud enough. As such, the simplest way to strengthen your clairaudience is to train your ears to be more sensitive in general.

This is best accomplished in a relaxing outdoor setting with as much natural sound as possible. Close your eyes so it's easier to focus on sound, reduce cross-sensory interference, and begin with breathing relaxation. With the intention of sensitizing your ears and deepening your psychic ability to hear beyond the physical world, focus as strongly as you can on making your hearing the main channel of input. Focus on as much detail as you can in the sounds around you, paying special attention to those sounds that you'd otherwise ignore. Try to unpack the soundscape into different layers or components while figuring out where each bit of sound is coming from. This will lend itself to imagination, so your visualization will be put to use as well.

What you want is to hear as much as possible while also developing your ability to discern as many different sounds as possible. Looking for layers in the sounds around you will make it easier to detect minute differences, which, in turn, strengthens your ability to intuitively tell sounds apart. As a result, you'll become more sensitive to both external and internal auditory cues. After a while, you'll gradually start hearing more than the average person, and it's only a matter of time until this translates into at least basic psychic abilities. As always, writing your observations down will enhance the exercise.

3. Clairsentience – Clear Feeling

The ability to follow your proverbial gut is one of the pillars of clairsentience. One way to enhance this clair is through basic exercises in empathy, especially those that mix in basic psychic abilities. A common exercise revolves around photographs of people, where you'll take a picture of someone you don't know while talking to someone who knows the person in the picture. Better yet, your partner could be someone who knows the person and has also taken the photograph in question. Observe the photograph and try to deduce as much as you can about this unknown person via your gut feeling alone. Focus on what kind of energy they're projecting in the picture, how they might be feeling, what they're like in general, et cetera. After a couple of minutes of guesswork, ask your partner how many of your guesses were correct.

On the physical side of clear feeling, energy-related exercises can boost your intuition tremendously. Any exercise that revolves around increasing your sensitivity to energetic shifts will do, including yoga, meditation, rituals against negative energy, and more. You should also learn as much as you can about your energy body, incorporating rituals that revolve around it into your daily routine. Advanced visualization exercises that have to do with energy, such as energy sphere visualizations, energy scans on yourself or others, and exercises related to your aura.

4. Claircognizance – Clear Knowing

Clear knowing is related to clear feeling because they both concern drawing conclusions from your intuition. They're both about trusting your gut, although clairsentience has a bit more to do with sensitivity to energies and is often focused on specific tasks or decisions that are at hand. In a way, it could be said that claircognizance is more chaotic. This is because it relies on thoughts, hunches, and instincts that seem to kick in at random.

Sometimes, you just have a "feeling" that you should or shouldn't do something, and it seems like little more than a hunch. Learning to trust this sense is essentially how you'll enhance your claircognizance. You can build up this trust by putting your intuition to the test, such as through the aforementioned empathy experiment with photographs. There are many other opportunities to test your claircognizance, however, and the more times your gut is proven right, the stronger it will become because it relies on the confidence you have in it.

Chapter 3: How to Connect with Your Spirit Guides

Now that you have a grasp on some basic spiritual concepts and practices and an understanding of what spiritual entities or guides are in essence, the path is open toward learning more about spirit guides. While reading their messages is often an intuitive exercise with many possible interpretations, many of these messages come in specific forms that have long been understood and studied by spiritual practitioners worldwide.

This chapter will provide you with a more thorough understanding of what spirit guides are in general and what exactly their messages look like. You will also learn about basic techniques that will help you grow your sensitivity to spiritual messages and increase your ability to interpret them correctly. Knowing more about the role of spirit guides entails learning ways of identifying their presence as well, which naturally precedes the skills needed to begin communication with them.

Connect with your spirit guides."

Understanding More About Spirit Guides

As briefly mentioned earlier, the concept of spirit guides is a very general one, usually serving as the umbrella term to include all the different entities described in this book. Each type of spirit guide has its own specific definition, as discussed in the first chapter, but defining the general concept is a somewhat different exercise. Because the idea of spiritual guardians and entities that communicate with the living has been so prevalent across different cultures, there are quite a few interpretations of this phenomenon.

In the interest of simplicity, you should view spirit guides as entities beyond the physical world who are there to help people in various ways, usually with subtlety. Spirit guides can also be classified into personal and ubiquitous guides, also known as working guides. In some practices, each person is believed to have one personal guide, while other traditions, particularly Eastern ones, stipulate that everyone has multiple entities watching over them throughout their lives. At the end of the day, the exact number of personal guides that you have won't matter once you master the art of reading their messages, as these skills will undoubtedly allow you to reach out to all of them.

Spirit guides are not there to solve all your problems for you, but they can help you fulfill your potential, make positive changes, overcome spiritual or emotional hardships, and much more. If chance permits, spirit guides can even help those who aren't necessarily listening to them or actively looking for their signs. While fortune can extend its hand with great results sometimes, putting in the effort to learn the language of spirit guides is guaranteed to yield rewards.

All of the spirit guides briefly covered earlier have unique characteristics and purposes. They each play their roles and excel at different forms of guidance. This is one of the reasons why some of these guides are more subtle than others and why contacting some of them might be more challenging than is the case with others. High-level guides like ascended masters will require more skill, psychic prowess, and ritualistic sophistication than your personal spirit guide or a departed loved one. This is because your relationship with the latter benefits from an intense personal bond, which opens up opportunities even for untrained, amateur mediums.

While spirit guides are entities in their own right, a lot of their spiritual messages come through you. In other words, the communication between you and a spirit guide doesn't necessarily occur outside of you. The guides themselves are external, but your intuitive realization and understanding of their messages occur within you. In a way, you are the window and portal through which spiritual messages come in from the other side, and they ultimately manifest inside your mind. This is why intuition and introspection play such important roles in spiritual communication.

Another thing that's essential to understand about spirit guides is that they respect free will and will rarely, if ever, directly intervene in worldly affairs. You shouldn't expect them to solve all your problems or take the reins of your life. Still, that doesn't mean they won't intervene at all. Rather, it means that they have their unique, often subtle ways of intervening, which you might initially misinterpret as underwhelming if your expectations are unrealistic. A spirit guide's intervention consists primarily of guidance, spiritual support, and important realizations in your life. They can and will show up in times of great need or even at your invitation, but you must never forget that you will always be the one who's firmly in charge of your life.

Channels of Spiritual Messaging

Spirit guides have many different avenues of communication, and their messages can come in some rather unexpected forms. While interpretation is an exercise in itself, understanding the ways in which spirit guides communicate is essential because you need to know what you're looking for. On top of that, not all types of spirit guides will communicate in the same way, even though there can be a fair amount of overlap. Some signs and symbols are mostly unique to respective entities, and differentiating between them plays a part in understanding the message. In general, identifying messages from spirit guides boils down to knowing where to look, noticing the signs, and knowing the kind of entity behind the message.

For many people, spirit messages come in when they're dreaming. As spirit messages, dreams can also be classified into the broader category of visions, although different kinds of visions exist. Visions can occur when you're awake, although this occurs with far less frequency, and most people will rarely have such experiences. The definition of what constitutes a vision is also somewhat loose, although they usually entail some kind of distinct realization that manifests visually.

Waking visions can happen at random, but those who get them will often be highly spiritual individuals engaged in meditation or a similar exercise. On the other hand, dreams are ubiquitous and provide a window into spiritual communications that virtually everyone can access. Some folks will dream more intensely than others and not everyone will recall their dreams with the same level of clarity, but remembering and recording your dreams is a skill that can be improved with practice.

On the more subtle side of things, spirit guides will communicate through things like thoughts, feelings, and sensations. This is where skills such as the four clairs truly come into their own because recognizing these subtle messages requires significant introspection, self-knowledge, and intuition. For instance, recognizing that one of your own conscious thoughts is a spirit message instead of just another thought can be incredibly difficult for the untrained mind. Only those with advanced intuition and sophisticated introspective skills will be able to pick apart their own thoughts and analyze the nuances. With feelings and spontaneous physical sensations, it's a bit easier to identify that they're coming from a spiritual source, but your four clairs still have to be sensitive.

Spirit guides will also sometimes communicate through something called intuitive nudges. An intuitive nudge occurs when you experience a seemingly inexplicable yet distinct urge to do something. It can come in the form of a mysterious attraction toward a certain course or a thought that seemingly crops up out of nowhere and pushes you toward a particular path. This nagging feeling that something should be done is something that a lot of people experience, yet many of them don't know that it could be a message from their spirit guide. These so-called nudges are highly intuitive, as is the decision process that helps you determine whether this nudge should be followed or suppressed.

There are also spirit messages that are much more overt and observable, even tangible at times, representing a distinct contrast to abstract signs such as those in dreams or intuition. Spirit guides might leave signs and symbols in the most unexpected places, which can include actual ancient symbols from various spiritual traditions, as you'll learn in subsequent chapters focusing on specific spirit guides. However, the symbols can also come in everyday items, including feathers, crystals, personal items, and much more. Animals can also be incredibly powerful symbols and carry all sorts of messages, which is why it's no accident that animal guides represent their own category.

Symbols can also come in the form of everyday items, which include feathers, crystals, personal items, and much more.⁹

While symbols like feathers are associated with entities like angels, their specific meaning and that of other objects will depend on the context in which you encounter them and your personal relationship with those objects. Lost items might show up at opportune times or in ways that convey a certain meaning, which you'll intuitively perceive as meaningful. The same holds true for other forms of spiritual messaging, such as sounds, smells, and tactile experiences. All of these messages exist in the physical world and are thus perceivable via your five senses, but just like feelings and thoughts, they can be interpreted only through intuition.

Last but not least, synchronicities are a major channel of communication with spirit guides. These are coincidental events where you notice a peculiar pattern, repetition, or coincidence that seems so meaningful that you are convinced it couldn't have been an accident. Thinking of a person just before you randomly run into them, having a brief vision of an event just before it happens, or having synchronized thoughts with someone are only some examples. Other synchronicities can include things like repetitive numbers, codes, colors, or anything else that seems to show up whenever you do or think a certain thing.

The ways in which these synchronicities appear are endlessly variable and can include anything that seems meaningful to you personally. Songs, phrases, sounds, smells, and many other occurrences can all be synchronous with other things in a way that gives you insight into what course you should take or reveal important truths. This is a textbook example of how a spiritual guide might be trying to get through to you.

Spiritual Communications and Connections 101

The exercises and tips discussed below will be foundational in allowing you to begin the process of spiritual connection. Think of them as entry-level skills and good practices that will be applicable to the more specific rituals that will be covered in the rest of the book with respect to specific kinds of spirit guides. These revolve around mental preparation, spiritual fortitude, meditation, and various routines that will enhance your receptivity to the spirit realm.

Setting Intentions

Your intentions will play a central role in all sorts of spiritual exercises. Whether in meditation, yoga, plain old prayer, or a complex esoteric ritual, setting a clear and powerful intention will be the driving force behind the effort. Remember that spiritual rituals are almost always about directing certain energies toward a goal, whether these energies are your own or external ones that you are trying to invoke and use. The intention behind the ritual is what you meditate on or use to visualize a desired result, which is why every ritual begins with an intention.

In spiritual communication, the basic intention is to establish contact with a spirit guide, receive a message, and have the clarity of mind and spirit needed to understand that message. Your intention should be firm, clear, articulate, and loving - or otherwise positive. The more positivity you project in your rituals, the more likely you are to attract a positive response from your spirit guides. The essence of the intention in the rituals you'll soon learn is to invite a spirit guide into your awareness.

Furthermore, intentions can be greatly enhanced in your rituals if you use things like affirmations, prayers, or mantras to articulate your intent. This is a way of verbalizing your goal to solidify its meaning and make it clearer both for yourself and the spirit guide you're trying to contact. Your affirmation can be anything you might think of, as long as it relates to the exercise at hand. For instance, if you're conducting a ritual aimed at receiving messages from a departed loved one, you can create your own special prayer or affirmation that resonates on a personal level.

Affirmations can also be conventional prayers or even excerpts from a poem, as long as they are relatable. One example of an affirmation directed at a spirit guide could be, "I invite my spirit guide to communicate with me for my highest good. I am open to your presence and guidance." This kind of verbal statement externalizes and clearly defines your intention, imbuing a ritual with powerful energy. Affirmations are used at the beginning of rituals or at various other points in the process, as you'll learn later when you go through some specific exercises.

Psychic Defense

To further solidify your spiritual foundation before communicating with guides, you could also look into techniques for psychic defense. Psychic defense and, similarly, spiritual protection are broad terms that describe an entire set of techniques and practices aimed at fortifying your spirit, energy, and mind against all sorts of negative influences. While spiritual communication isn't inherently dangerous, it doesn't hurt to build basic psychic defenses to make your mind and energy invulnerable to any potential interference. These can include false, unwanted entities like pseudo-guides or negative energy attached to you by other people, whether unwittingly or through deliberate psychic attacks.

It's about more than just protection because psychic defenses will inevitably accentuate your psychic abilities as well, helping you see spirit messages more clearly and understand them more easily. Basic psychic defense is very straightforward and can consist of simple exercises like meditation, daily affirmations, prayer, energy-cleansing rituals, and more. Aura shielding can be especially effective, allowing you to build a protective energetic layer around your aura to make your energy impervious to unwanted external effects. You can shield your aura by using shielding crystals that project a protective field, shielding visualizations, positive affirmations, and numerous other methods. Physical changes in your lifestyle, such as healthy diets and regular exercise, can also strengthen your aura and will always have positive effects on your spirituality.

Meditation to Meet Your Spirit Guide

Trying to get in touch with your spirit guide through meditation is a common approach, and it'll depend on the power of your intention and your ability to visualize and focus. Refer to what you learned about sacred mental spaces in the previous chapter before you begin this process. Meditation to meet your spirit guide can be as simple or as complex as you wish it to be. It always revolves around visualization and mental effort, but the amount of time and effort you put into it will determine if it's a quick evening routine or a full-blown shamanic journey. The latter can also be conducted under the guidance of a professional psychic.

After you enter a state of relaxation and return to that special sacred place in your mind, you will have to engage in sophisticated visualization to get to your goal. Once you're in your sacred space, start by visualizing it, taking on a different, more complex form. Imagine a natural environment that inspires calm, connectedness, and beauty. Try to get as immersed as your mind is capable of, imagining the physical sensation of being there. Focus on specific details of this imagined space to make it feel more realistic, such as its colors, sounds, and smells. Imagine smelling the scents as you breathe in and out.

You can meet your spirit guides through visualization and focus during meditation.[10]

Next, imagine a path or stairway that leads upward to the sky, once again focusing on as many details as possible. These details can include visible things like divine light but also realizations and feelings, such as those telling you that this path leads toward discovery and enlightenment. Start a mental journey on this path and picture each step as bringing you closer to the realm of spirits and guidance, all while feeling a change in the surrounding energies.

Focus on the energy of this place as hard as you can and gradually visualize it turning into a feeling of some kind of presence beside you. Intensify this feeling and imagine yourself turning to your side, beholding a figure of pure blissful light and benevolent radiance. Imagine this as your spirit guide, and let each breath reveal a sensation of absorbing this loving energy. Try to attribute characteristics and traits to this figure, including wisdom, benevolence, compassion, and understanding. Focus on feeling a powerful personal bond to this being, making yourself feel as if you're greeting a lifelong friend or companion.

The only thing that then remains is to have a mental conversation and a spiritual exchange with this powerful entity. Ask the questions that trouble you and use your intuition to understand the answers. It's important to show gratitude as well, which you can do by visualizing yourself presenting a gift to your spirit guide or using a physical object as a ritualistic offering. The final stage of the meditation boils down to visualizing your way back home by following the same pathway you came through. Visualize your spirit guide following you as you leave and bidding you farewell until your next meeting.

As you can see, this is a complex meditative exercise that will require tremendous mental work and focus. The more steps you take to make your meditation more comforting and ritualistic, the easier it will be to rid your mind of distractions. Every time you finish such rituals, you should take time to reflect on the things you realized, felt, and thought, writing them down and analyzing the results. Allow yourself some time to let the impressions settle and become integrated.

Journaling

Identifying and understanding spirit messages often has a lot to do with recognizing patterns and referring to previous experiences when facing new information. Keeping a journal is one of the best tools available for these purposes. As briefly mentioned earlier, writing things down solidifies your thoughts, strengthens visualization, and makes it much easier for you to identify patterns.

Half the effort consists of writing in your journal, while the other half is about regularly studying your writings and referencing them as you try to identify new signs from your spirit guides. Your journal should focus on signs, symbols, synchronicities, feelings, random thoughts, or anything else you believe might be connected with a spirit guide. Since spirit message interpretation tends to be personal, only you will know, through your intuition, which signs are worth recording. Consider the following prompts as a general idea of the kinds of observations you should be making, in addition to writing down the details of your experiences in actual rituals:

Have I experienced any feelings today that seemed to come out at random, without a clearly identifiable source, and unrelated to any specific event?

Which of today's events felt peculiar in the sense that they seemed inexplicably connected to something else through sheer coincidence?

Did I encounter any objects that appeared in places where they didn't belong or somehow provoked an emotional response that felt meaningful for reasons that are difficult to explain?

Was my attention grabbed by any specific symbols I've seen, and how did they make me feel? What is the meaning of these symbols?

Automatic Writing

Automatic writing is a technique that can enhance a number of specific spiritual communication rituals while also having some more general benefits in your daily life. It's a simple exercise that revolves around unfiltered, non-stop expression through pen and paper for a certain interval. The nature of the exercise is such that it can provide a whole lot of text, so it's a good idea to designate a specific part of your journal or have an entire notebook dedicated to automatic writing.

After you prepare a pen and notebook, all you have to do is pick a theme that works best in the form of a question. The question should ideally be one that a spiritual guide might help you with, referring to the kind of guidance you need or the solution for a particular problem. Once you set the question firmly in your mind, you'll attempt to answer it yourself. Take a timer and set it to an interval of your choosing, perhaps no more than twenty minutes.

The moment you let the timer loose, start writing continuously, letting everything that comes to your mind onto the paper. Let your pen function as a free-flowing conduit to every thought, impulse, idea, or feeling that your mind might conjure up, and try to let your brain wander as much as possible while keeping your question in focus. Try not to think about what you're writing, and don't try to keep the grammar or punctuation clean. You want to produce a torrent of spontaneous thoughts that are externalized on paper in as raw of a state as possible. Once you're done, you should take some time to analyze your writing.

Try to understand how some of the thoughts formed and where they came from. The exercise aims to let your intuition run wild and learn how to trust it. Automatic writing can also do wonders for your claircognizance by strengthening your so-called gut feeling. You should also try to identify which of the thoughts in your notebook were conscious and which weren't. Among the latter is where you're most likely to find a message from a spiritual source. As a result, automatic writing will also improve your ability to differentiate between your thoughts and those incepted by your spirit guides.

Strengthening the Connection

As with any other spiritual practice, communicating with your spirit guide will benefit greatly from the regular effort that's incorporated into some sort of routine. This includes rituals aimed specifically at spiritual communication as well as general exercises to keep your energy in balance. Morning routines can be especially important because they can set the right mindset that will positively affect the rest of your day. As you learn about more rituals throughout the rest of the chapters, you'll be able to decide which rituals concerning your spirit guides are the simplest or most applicable to your usual routine, allowing you to create a tailored approach that best suits your needs.

In general, it's good practice to begin your day with at least some basic meditation involving breath awareness and brief check-ins with your spirit guide. Grounding meditation is also an excellent way to start your day if your living conditions and location allow it. You should also remember to practice gratitude throughout your day in whatever way you see fit, particularly toward your spirit guides. Small symbolic offerings or meditative reflections at a basic altar dedicated to your spirit guides will deepen your bond and facilitate a healthy and positive mindset.

Whenever you can, take a moment to reflect on the guidance you have already received from the spirits, expressing gratitude for it and a hope for their continued assistance in the future.

Chapter 4: Connecting with Your Animal Guides and Totems

Now that you've got a solid grasp on basic spiritual work and the essential concepts behind spirit guides, it's time to delve deeper into the various forms that spirit guides take. This chapter will focus on animal spirit guides and the adjacent topic of animal totems, which feature various similarities but also a number of key differences. Both of these separate concepts include powerful symbolism and revolve around the inherent human connection to facets of the natural world, in this case, animals.

Spirit guides can come in an animal form.[11]

Across this and the following chapter, you will find that nature abounds in spirits, messages, and guidance, waiting to be unlocked by a spiritually curious mind. You will soon learn more about what animal guides and totems are, what messages they might have for you, and how to read them. These mighty spiritual allies that assume the form of animals are diverse and are always at work to help people, but you have to know how to listen to their guidance.

Animal Guides and Totems

One of the key differences that set animal guides apart from other spirit guides is that they can take a form that's clearly observable in the physical world. Even if they are encountered indirectly, such as in a dream or vision, animal guides still assume a form that's familiar to the human mind. Animals are an essential part of the natural world and, as such, have played many crucial roles in the human experience since the very beginning.

This deeply rooted familiarity is what has facilitated a certain level of understanding that humans have for animals despite the many ways in which they differ from each other. It has also imbued animals with great importance in the lives of people, which has translated into spirituality time and time again. Animals act as powerful symbols, and how they look, behave, and interact with humans has always been given a lot of meaning across different cultures.

The first step toward harnessing the power of animal guides and totems is to understand what makes them different. As briefly mentioned, a spiritual animal guide can be seen as an entity that takes the shape of an animal to convey certain meanings to people. As an entity that resides in the spiritual realm, an animal guide might come into your life in specific situations or when you're facing a particular challenge. Animal guides can communicate warnings, lessons, and all manner of wisdom, often related to the natural traits and instincts of the animal in question.

On the other hand, an animal totem, sometimes also referred to as your power animal, should be seen as a lifelong companion and protector, meaningful to you on a deeply personal level. The concept of animal totems is usually associated with Native American culture and is steeped in thousands of years of tradition that's intensely focused on the human spiritual relationship with nature and the animal kingdom. Your animal totem or power animal is your personal natural protector and companion that serves as a conduit between you and nature, symbolizing some of your essential characteristics. It can be a symbol of your essential identity and spiritual power and is tied to your deepest values and the path you walk in life.

As a symbolic representation of your essence in animal form, your animal totem can be interpreted as your spirit and essential self. As per some Native American traditions, an individual can have as many as nine animal totems. Discovering your personal animal totems is a deeply introspective exercise in which you must be sensitive to how you feel and think about certain animals. Experiences with those animals can also be meaningful and indicative of a special relationship. If a certain kind of animal seems to follow you everywhere you go, whether in dreams or in your waking hours, it might be your power animal. Being spontaneously approached by such an animal and being shown trust by them is also a powerful confirmation of a bond.

As your highly personal symbol or emblem, your animal totem's meaning can be quite flexible. Across cultures, different animals have their unique, innate symbolisms, but an animal totem's essential power is still in the way it relates to you personally. For instance, dragonflies are generally seen as signs of good luck, while butterflies often represent transformation and change, but that doesn't mean they'll necessarily represent the same things for everyone. The main importance of your animal totem will be in the traits, strengths, weaknesses, and inclinations that you and that animal share.

How Animal Guides Communicate

In regard to animal spirit guides and how they might communicate with you, there will be some signs that they share with other spirit guides. Other signs will be specific to the animal kingdom as a whole or to individual animal species. As mentioned earlier, recurrence is an essential sign. The more often you see an animal, whether in person or in a vision or dream, the more likely it is that an animal guide is trying to communicate with you.

These animal spirits might appear in their full form, but they can also communicate through traces hinting at their presence. The animal guide's choice between the former and the latter can also hold a meaningful message in itself. For example, repeatedly seeing a hawk or just finding its feathers without seeing the actual bird can be an important distinction. An animal spirit guide might have its reasons for being intentionally elusive toward you while deliberately leaving a trail of small hints to let you know that they are present. Bits of fur, horns, or tracks are also common signals with which animal spirit guides can communicate, indicating that you are following their trail in the wild or that they routinely visit places where you often find yourself in life.

To identify animal guides and understand their messages, it's also crucial to understand the behavior, habitat, and other natural characteristics of individual animals. Knowing these things will make it easier to discern whether an animal's presence in a given location is a mere coincidence or something more. The same goes for the symbolism of different animals across spiritual traditions, which you should extensively study once you identify which animals tend to make a recurring entrance in your life.

For example, consider how an owl lives and what it represents. An owl is a nighttime hunter who tends to dwell in forests or near them, symbolizing things like wisdom, powerful vision, and intuition in many cultures. If you find yourself taking an evening walk on a forest trail and you hear or see an owl, this may or may not be a meaningful encounter. On the other hand, if an owl visits your suburban home at noon or - *stranger yet* - shows up in an urban environment, the likelihood that this is just chance will be much smaller.

Because of its strong association with wisdom and insight, a spirit guide in the form of an owl might emerge at a time when you need guidance and wise reflection regarding an important decision. Taking into account the place and time of this encounter, as well as the thoughts and feelings that it sparks within you, such a meeting could produce an intuitive nudge or overtly reveal to you the path that you should take. The combinations of circumstances and subtle signs that might accompany an animal encounter offer a virtually limitless array of ways for spirit guides to communicate via animals. At the end of the day, the true meaning behind these encounters will only be unlocked through your own intuition and deep reflection.

Connecting with Animal Guides

To understand the messages you might be getting through animal guides, you'll generally analyze physical encounters with certain animals or read into synchronicities associated with those animals. Animals might appear repeatedly not just as a physical presence but also as images, visions, dreams, or thoughts. Apart from passively observing and analyzing such clues, you can also take a more proactive approach through some of the exercises described below.

Connecting via Meditation

As is often the case, meditation is a powerful venue for wandering into the spirit realm, and it's no different with animal spirits. However, connecting with an animal guide via meditation can be particularly tricky and requires a fair amount of practice. This is because the skittish nature of animals can often carry over into their spirits as well, so they aren't always rushing to talk to people.

As always, the meditation starts with an intention; in this case, the idea of having an animal guide reveals itself. This can be the spirit of an animal that fascinates or frequently visits you, or it can be the spirit of a departed pet. After setting your intention, you will move on to your usual meditative position and begin a process of visualization. Don't set high expectations or overthink the process, and don't try to analyze what you see. The goal is to simply conjure up the animal in the eye of your mind.

Connect to your animal guides by meditating.[13]

Visualize a walk along a path in the forest or somewhere else that's comfortable and serene. Without analyzing anything, let the sights, sounds, and smells of this place conjure up in your mind, and just observe. As you walk down this path, imagine that you are coming upon a place of transition into the realm of spirits. This can be a doorway, bridge, or anything else that symbolizes crossing over to another side. Before crossing over, reinforce your intention to meet an animal spirit guide and formulate it as a humble request. Assure yourself that a guide wants to meet you and will be waiting on the other side, and then gradually cross.

Visualize yourself coming across a figure in the distance, fitting seamlessly into a natural landscape before you. Imagine this figure as small and distant at first – but gradually getting closer. This will be your animal guide.

As the meeting draws nearer, visualize more and more details of this ethereal animal and allow it to dictate the tempo of the encounter. Depending on the kind of animal guide you're meeting and your goals, you will, at this point, ask the questions that you want to ask, all while maintaining an intense meditative state.

Animal Guide Journaling

Like most other forms of spiritual communication, keeping a journal can greatly help. It will help you keep a record of all suspected spirit messages, whether real or not, and allow you to reference them in retrospect. This is essential if you are to notice the patterns and synchronicities that so often accompany these messages. It's all about collecting as much data as possible and then processing it gradually. The more things that you write down, the more nuanced and perceptive your efforts at identifying animal guide messages will become.

A journal or a part of a journal dedicated to animal guides would be rather simple. Your main focus would be on recurring symbols, signs, and encounters associated with animals. The animals that hold a higher degree of meaning for you should get the most attention, of course, but any recurring instances can be important even if they don't feature the animals that you're most interested in.

You can start by making a journal note of every time you see a symbol or sign connected to an animal or any physical encounter, for about a month. When you start writing everything down, you'll find that many instances in daily life are brushed off or simply forgotten, making it more difficult to identify patterns and recurrences. Writing down every instance and reviewing your journal every day is the quickest way to figure out which animals are repeatedly showing up in your life.

As always, make sure that you also record the things you felt or thought during particular encounters. When you review your journal thoroughly at the end of the month, you might find that certain animals show up quite frequently and are accompanied by sensations, feelings, thoughts, intuitive nudges, and much more. If you notice repetitions both in the encounters and the accompanying features, you can be fairly certain that an animal guide is at work.

Using Animal Oracle Cards

Animal oracle cards can be of great use as a means of drawing hints and inspiration from the animal world, but they can also help you identify which guides you are most inclined toward. These cards, which can be bought or even made if you're feeling creative, mostly revolve around animal symbolism and are meant to explore your connections with certain animals. All you need is a deck of oracle cards, a quiet space, and a journal where you can document your discoveries and messages. The main benefits of using animal oracle cards include strengthened intuition, emotional processing, and life insights.

The simplest way to use a deck of oracle cards is to sit down in your meditative space and set an intention, usually a question or an issue where you need guidance. Focus your energy on your objective and shuffle the deck while continuously reflecting on your intention.

Once you've thoroughly mixed up the cards, you can draw a card and see what it tells you. You can draw this card at random or try to intuitively feel which card you're most drawn to, and you can repeat this process with multiple cards for a more detailed reading. To use your card deck to identify which animal's spirit resonates with you the most, it's a good idea to indulge in some repetition to see which animal card seems to show up more than others.

You can try different spreads and layouts for a more complex reading, such as a basic three-card spread. This spread is frequently used to gain insights into your past, present, and future, which the three cards will represent. The idea is to interpret how the past connects to the present and influences your current circumstances and the events yet to come.

Getting in Touch with Your Animal Totem

Connecting with your animal totem is all about identifying it and strengthening your bond with that particular animal symbol. It's an exercise in reflection, introspection, meditation, prayer, and much more, with the ultimate goal of drawing inspiration and spiritual strength from your power animal. As such, it's a spiritual endeavor that's considerably different from receiving animal guide messages because it boils down to finding a bond that already exists and then exploring it for your spiritual benefit.

The main benefit of intensifying the bond with your animal totem is that it'll help you align with your spiritual path and, hopefully, unlock hidden strengths and qualities within you that you didn't know existed. It's all about honoring your animal protector and getting in touch with the traits and strengths that this animal symbolizes through its nature and characteristics. Below, you'll find a few examples of how you can deepen this connection with an animal totem and, by extension, nature as a whole.

Animal Totem Quest

An animal totem quest, in this case, a shamanic journey through the spirit world, is a fairly complex meditative exercise meant to help you meet your animal totem and strengthen the bond between you. It's about journeying through the three main spirit worlds of shamanic cosmology, which include the lower, middle, and upper worlds.

These three worlds are usually interpreted as making up the proverbial tree of life and representing the tree's roots, trunk, and branches, respectively. The lower world is the residence of animals and other nature spirits, in humans associated with the unconscious mind and psychology.

Animal totems.[18]

The middle world is the realm of human beings, both those who are alive and those whose spirits refuse to move on to the spirit realm. It's associated with basic survival instincts but also the human desire to transcend and find meaning in the universe. Lastly, the upper world is the world of higher spiritual entities, especially guides like angels, the ascended masters, and other high beings.

To take this shamanic journey, you should try and induce a trance-like state, which is the basis of many shamanic rituals. This is usually done with a set of drums because rhythmic drumming, particularly at a rate of three to four beats per second, facilitates a state of trance. The same holds true for a variety of repetitive sounds, but drums are the traditional tool of choice for shamans. Doing the drumming yourself will be more immersive, but recordings of shamanic drumming found on the Internet can do the trick as well. Inducing a shamanic trance is no easy task for beginners, of course, so it will require a lot of practice and intense concentration.

The journey is best done by lying down comfortably for up to 30 minutes immersed in shamanic drumming. You can conduct this ritual in darkness or cover your eyes to minimize distractions.

As with regular meditation, begin by using your breathing to enter a state of relaxation. Similar to the previously discussed meditation ritual, visualize a natural place for your journey. This time, however, look for a hole in the ground or in a tree trunk and imagine it as an animal's den. This is where you'll enter and begin your descent toward the lower world. To vividly picture the downward journey, imagine yourself following the roots of a tree.

When you're ready, visualize yourself suddenly emerging from the ground and entering a vast, open space. Although this foreign place may look like the middle world of humanity, it will actually be the lower world. Imagine as many features and your own feelings as possible to make the place as real as you can in your mind. Observing the natural wonders of this place, you should eventually begin meeting animals. The first animal you see will rarely be your exact animal totem, but don't hesitate to ask. These other animals can also lead you to your guide.

Once you find the animal spirit that you're seeking, spend some time with it and get to know each other. Ask questions about the animal itself before moving on to asking for the answers that you came seeking. This is also where you can ask your animal spirit to take you on a quest around its realm and create whatever story you please. Shamanic drum recordings usually have different sections to guide your journey. Once it comes to the part featuring slow thumping, the journey should gradually come to a close as you return back to your realm.

Visualize yourself returning the same way you came, along the roots and through the tunnel, and only then allow yourself to emerge back in your room. Remember to make a journal entry that goes into the details of your journey, which will give you something to analyze and also help you make future journeys more intense and vivid as your mind gets used to the idea.

Bonding with Your Animal Totem

Strengthening your bond with your animal totem or spirit animal can and should be an ongoing effort that you can incorporate into your daily routine and spiritual practices. The simplest and most accessible method would be to study your preferred animal in as much detail as you can. This means turning a certain animal into a part of your life, particularly those of its qualities that you admire and draw inspiration from.

Learn as much as you can about the animal's habits, environment, innate traits, and instincts. The more you learn about the animal, the closer you'll feel to it, and you'll find that all of the animal's behaviors, characteristics, and way of life are full of powerful symbolism that you can relate to.

You can also take up various small rituals centered on honoring your animal totem. One way to do this is to build an altar in your animal's honor. Apart from fostering your creativity and providing some interesting decor in your home, an altar will serve as a place of reflection and meditation that you can use as a spiritual retreat. Your animal totem's altar will also be a place where you can give offerings to your power animal in the form of items and symbols that you associate with it. Symbolic items that represent a spirit animal can also be placed elsewhere throughout your home to ward off negative energy and symbolize your natural source of strength and inspiration.

Animal Dance and Movement

Last but not least, you can also strengthen the bond with your animal totem through your physical body. This is also a way for you to try and physically integrate some of the animal's power. It boils down to embodying the energy of your totem by adjusting your physical movements and stature to mimic the movements and natural positions of a certain animal. Of course, this doesn't mean walking around like an animal in your daily life. Rather, it's about assuming certain positions and making movements as part of some of your rituals, particularly when you're meditating or visualizing.

This can also be done during nature walks if you choose to meditate in nature as a way of getting even closer to animal guides and totems. Walking meditations, for instance, are powerful grounding rituals that are sure to make you more present in nature, which will also inevitably approximate you with animal spirits. The next chapter, which is all about nature spirits, will go into much more detail on connecting with nature on a spiritual level.

Chapter 5: Messages from Nature Spirits

For a lot of people, animals are the first association when nature is mentioned, but nature is home to many other spiritual entities. In some cultures, learning directly from nature is one of the central aspects of human life, and such ideas are deeply entrenched in their religious and spiritual practices. The harmony between nature and human beings is of great importance across cultures and civilizations, regardless of how much of their worship is focused explicitly on nature.

You can receive spiritual messages through nature as well.[14]

Because of their diversity, nature spirits are a somewhat broad term that describes a number of different spirit guides, entities, and concepts. Nature's wisdom is carried by spirits that inhabit trees, spiritual entities like fairies, the four elements of the natural world, and much more.

This chapter will provide you with some deeper insights into what nature spirits are, their types, how they influence the natural environment, and how they might be communicating with you. It will also feature a handful of practical exercises and tips that you can use to deepen your connection with nature, sharpening your eyes and ears to the things nature can tell you.

Understanding Nature Spirits

To start with, it's worth mentioning that many classifications will put animal spirits into the category of nature spirits, which is certainly where they belong. The reason why animal guides and spirits are often treated as practically separate is that animals themselves are incredibly diverse and have played such a prominent cultural role for many millennia. With that being said, nature spirits beyond animals are still quite diverse and numerous, covering many aspects of nature that you can see, feel, and imagine.

Apart from already mentioned spirits like those of trees and fairies, some of the other natural spirits that can be found scattered across spiritual traditions include gnomes, sylphs, nymphs, elves, mermaids, and many others. The number of these fantastical creatures seen as representing nature and her processes is matched only by the diversity of cultures and traditions that have observed and revered the natural world.

While the indigenous traditions of America are famous for their reverence of spirit animals and totems, there are also other ancient takes on nature worship that are fairly familiar to the modern Western world. Celtic traditions and various shamanic teachings elsewhere in the world have also left behind teachings and views on the reverence of nature that are studied and practiced to this day. In ancient Celtic culture, the people's relationship with nature was inseparably intertwined with spirituality.

The old Celts believed wholeheartedly in an entire world or realm of spirits existing in parallel with the physical world and being every bit as real, regardless of the limitations of human senses. The Celtic god Cernunnos, for instance, was intimately associated with nature and regarded as the "lord of wild things." He was a god imbued with serenity, peace, and benevolence, portrayed visually as a human figure sporting a set of antlers and being surrounded by animals of various kinds. Being right with this deity was the way in which many ancient Celts sought to maintain harmony and balance with the natural world, with Cernunnos as an intermediary or incarnation of nature.

Perhaps more famously, the loosely defined traditions of shamanism are all about the natural world as something sacred, deeply spiritual, or even alive. According to various shamanic practices, spirits and spiritual energies permeate nature, and interacting with them through rituals and trances is a central aspect of human life. Shamans communicate with natural spirits on a deeper level, hoping to redirect their spiritual energies toward the benefit of human spirituality or health. In shamanism, virtually every aspect of nature is imbued with a living spirit, which includes animals, elements, plants, rivers, mountains, and other features observable to the human senses. Shamans might consider these features of nature to be living, spiritual beings in their own right, possessing consciousness and playing their roles in nature while also offering to teach wisdom to humans.

For the purposes of communicating with nature spirits, elemental spirits represent one of the most important categories. These spirits can be seen as embodiments of earth, air, water, and fire. Interpretations of such spiritual entities vary across traditions, but the four elements consistently play an important role in rituals aimed at spiritual and energy work. This is why rituals and altars in many esoteric practices usually feature some kind of symbolic representation for each of the elements.

The elements are seen as coming together to form the natural world, but each of the four is embodied by a set of spirits with unique properties and associations. This is why those who seek to communicate with elemental spirits might sometimes focus on the spirits connected to one or two elements instead of all at once. For instance, earth spirits tend to be associated with grounding and energetic stability, in addition to fertility and growth. Those looking to feel more centered in their direction while fostering a sense of stable grounding might seek the assistance of Earth spirits. These are usually the first spirits a practitioner will look for if their aim is to achieve a more intimate connection with the natural world.

Air spirits are all about movement and shifts, which often translates into matters related to energy and its flow in the natural world. These are highly communicative spirits who can provide a sense of clarity and stimulate the intellectual pursuits of the practitioner. They offer fresh perspectives on problems and situations in life, allowing people to analyze the details and find solutions through clarity of mind. On the other hand, the spirits of fire can be intense and inspire passion while representing transformation and fostering people's creativity. Communicating with fire spirits can invigorate you and increase your drive to achieve goals while increasing your vitality and readiness to effect change in your life.

Water elemental spirits are much calmer, having to do with your emotions and intuition. They also represent healing and flow in the broadest sense, with a penchant to interact with the deeper, subconscious recesses of your mind. If you're looking for inner wisdom or want to become better at processing your emotions, Water Spirits can provide tremendous guidance in that regard. All of these elemental spirits consistently influence the world in the realms of humans and spirits alike. Getting closer to these spirits entails deepening your relationship with nature on the most fundamental level since the elements themselves are nature's building blocks.

How Nature Spirits Communicate

The wisdom and inspiration in nature is found in all the little things you begin to notice once you become truly mindful, present, and grounded in a natural environment. These are things that most people normally don't notice because they are preoccupied with other pursuits as they go about their day. Listening to nature with every fiber of your being and being attentive to its finer processes on an intuitive level is the essence of communicating with nature spirits and heeding their guidance. This takes some effort, however, and it might even be considered a skill, but it's a skill that can be acquired quite easily.

Nature spirits are sure to communicate with you if you spend time outdoors and make an effort to listen to them. Channels of communication for these spirits can be incredibly diverse and will depend a lot on personal preferences. Essentially, any activity that you intuitively feel brings you closer to nature will enable you to communicate with its spirits. As is often the case with spiritual guidance, the insights and wisdom will come through the things you feel on the inside.

Nature spirits can also come to you at home, such as in your dreams or recurring symbols, signs, and feelings.[15]

Still, nature spirits will communicate in a lot of the ways that other spirit guides will. Any synchronicity that you observe when you're in nature can be highly meaningful and provide insights. Nature spirits can also come to you at home, such as in your dreams or recurring symbols, signs, and feelings. For instance, people will sometimes be consumed by visions of a particular place in the woods or elsewhere in the great outdoors, feeling inexplicably drawn to it. Such intuitive nudges should always be heeded and explored whenever the opportunity presents itself. You should also keep in mind the important role that animals and their spirits play in nature. Although animal guides are their own category, they will still sometimes interact with other nature spirits and participate in complex messages sent to you by nature.

Nature spirits can also make their presence known through all sorts of subtle or overt signs that seem only physical at first. Keep an eye out for abrupt changes in weather, feelings of a presence, or any kind of pattern you might notice in nature. The spirits will always be all around you when you enter an undisturbed natural location, but how, when, and if they're going to reach out to you directly can hardly be anticipated or preempted. The best thing to do is to just spend time within nature and open your mind and heart to its vibrations.

Hearing Nature Spirits More Clearly

To become more adept at listening to the messages that nature spirits offer, the most important thing you must do is strengthen your connection to nature. This doesn't just include seeking out specific nature spirits and guides. In a more general sense, you should find ways to become one with nature and immerse yourself in it in ways that too few people try these days. This means being physically and mentally present outdoors, spending time in nature, and engaging in various forms of meditation in environments that retain at least a moderate degree of their natural form.

Nature Walking Meditation

Engaging in meditation while taking a nature walk, also known as mindful walking, is a rather simple exercise. It's all about setting an intention to connect with nature or its spirits and doing your best to remain mentally and spiritually present while walking in a natural setting, ideally a forest. Make sure your steps are small and relaxed and that you're not rushing along the path. Keep your hands loose at your sides, and just let your body do its work automatically as you walk.

As usual, begin your meditation by focusing on your breathing and just observing it without thinking too much. A meditative walk in nature works best if you try not to think about and analyze your environment in any detail. This can be difficult because forests tend to overload the senses, but if you maintain focus on your breathing like you've learned to do, you'll get the hang of it. Continue observing your breathing and the way the air flows through you, energizing your body.

Once you're fully relaxed and walking spontaneously, slowly shift your focus to the way your feet interact with the soil beneath you. Maintain an awareness of this contact and gradually focus entirely on your steps, making sure to savor every sensation. Finally, you can begin to shift focus toward your environment by observing what you see, hear, and smell as impartially as possible. Use your senses as a new area of focus and when you're ready, try to visualize the nature spirits present in everything around you.

Nature Listening Meditation

The ambient sounds are one of the most stimulating aspects of a forest environment. This is why listening to nature can be so therapeutic and offers an excellent basis for meditation, especially with the goal of connecting to nature and hearing its spirits. It would work almost the same as a meditative nature walk, with the only difference being your focal point during meditation.

First, follow the same process until you arrive at a point where your focus shifts toward the environment and your actions during a walk. At that point, instead of focusing on the connection between your feet and the ground and all of your senses, set a narrower focus on the things you hear. Use your breathing as a focal point in case your mind begins to wander, and allow the sound of your breath to fuse with the ambient noises of the forest. Listen attentively and for as long as you can until you get a sharp picture of all the sounds around you, which will allow you to notice any sudden changes.

Any unusual sound, such as rustling or shifts in the wind, might carry messages from nature spirits if you listen closely enough. Don't hesitate to ask questions when paying attention to unusual noises, as you never know when an answer might come. You should also be on the lookout for any signs and symbols you might encounter, no matter how subtle. Keep your intention to hear nature spirits firmly in the back of your mind at all times.

Tree Spirit Meditation

Similarly, you can focus on specific nature spirits when you're out in the woods. Tree spirits are some of the most plentiful nature spirits in forested areas, so you can start there. It would work similarly to other forms of simple outdoor meditation, except that this time, you won't be walking. You should find a tree you feel drawn to, ideally one with a striking appearance and distinct characteristics. Meditation based on such a tree's spirit would work like most other meditations, but it would be based on the intention to connect with the tree's spirit.

Simply sit or stand close to the tree and enter a state of relaxation as you gradually begin visualizing the energy and spirits that permeate the tree from its roots and up to its branches. Focus on the idea that this tree is a living being like any other creature in the forest, with a powerful spirit coursing through it. Try to listen to the tree's sounds as the wind rustles its leaves or branches creak. Visualize a hidden world of thoughts and feelings within the tree and all of the things it would have witnessed over its long life. Open your mind and listen intently while also keeping an eye on your feelings, taking note of any sudden thoughts, sensations, or ideas that you might get.

Elemental Communication Ritual

Because the four basic elements of the world are such important aspects of nature, they're also a good channel of communication with nature spirits. Your elemental communication ritual can be anything you want it to be, with varying levels of complexity. You can indulge in elaborate rituals at an altar, using all sorts of esoteric materials to symbolize the elements, or you can simply seek to get closer to nature's elements by spending time with them outdoors.

For instance, sitting next to a river or a campfire is one of the best ways to meditate on the elements of water and fire. It will be much easier to visualize the spirit in things like rivers and crackling fires than it would be in a tree because of the obviously powerful energy that you can readily observe in these things. Similarly, you can observe the elemental spirits of air by listening to the endless cacophony of sounds that the wind produces, especially in the woods. Getting in touch with Elemental Earth is also easy if you walk barefoot.

Connect to Earth by walking barefoot.[16]

In general, any day you spend out in nature can be turned into an elaborate elemental communication ritual if you focus on the right things. If you observe and listen to the elements like you've never done before, you'll uncover a whole new world that you've been missing. If you ask the right questions while at it, you might find just the answers you were looking for in a dash of wind, the rumbling of a river, or the lights and shadows cast by a dancing fire at a campsite.

Creating a Nature Spirit Altar

To get closer to nature and its spirits in your spiritual pursuits, you can also build a nature spirit altar in a similar way that you would with an animal spirit or animal totem. The similarity is in the intention behind the altar because its intention will be to honor a particular nature spirit that you're most interested in. As such, your altar should feature as many symbols of that specific nature spirit as possible. It can also be a more generalized altar for all your rituals related to nature, featuring natural objects like leaves, stones, moss, feathers, or anything else you find when you're out and about.

It's also a good idea to include symbols and other representations of mythical creatures or deities found in Native American culture, ancient Celtic religion, shamanism, or other spiritual systems focused on nature. The great thing about altars is that they're so modular and adaptable, so there will be a lot of room for you to put a personal spin on it. Items of personal value are always a welcome addition as well, especially if they're related to nature, your memories associated with nature, or an outdoor place that's especially meaningful for you. Remember to also include symbolic representations of the four elements, such as soil, candles, water, and anything that might symbolize air or the wind.

Moonlight and Fairy Communication

Summoning entities like fairies is an advanced visualization exercise, but with enough focus and a proper setting, you might be able to master the art through practice. It's important to take note of the associations that these entities have with aspects of the natural world to maximize your chances. Fairies, for instance, are commonly associated with moonlight, so the best time to try and communicate with them is during a full moon.

At a comfortable, quiet place outdoors, position yourself in a moonlit spot and establish a baseline meditative state for visualization. Use the energy of the white light showering down from the moon to visualize the light as a pathway to the realm of fairies. You can try to either visualize fairies or simply the hidden world that they inhabit. Ask questions and focus on any unusual sounds that stick out in your quiet nighttime surroundings. If you focus the power of your visualization, you might eventually hear a soft whisper or experience feelings of warmth and presence.

Chapter 6: Angel Signs and Communication

Although they don't take on physical forms in a way that animal guides or other nature spirits might do, angelic entities are among the most frequently contacted spirit guides. Angels or entities similar to them feature prominently in many religions despite their usual association with Christianity. As you've learned earlier, angelic spirit guides come in various forms and are often separated into two main groups, including personal guardian angels and those who ubiquitously wander different realms, contacting various people.

Angels and archangels, whether they are your guardians since birth or come into your life occasionally, can provide much comfort and reassurance. Their messages are supportive, wise, and inspiring. This chapter will teach you more about the various angelic entities in the spirit realm and how they might be communicating with you. You will also get insights into a few practical exercises and tips that will surely help you identify more signs and strengthen your bond with whatever angels are fluttering around in your life.

Angelic Beings and Their Roles

In the broadest sense, angels as a whole can be considered protective spiritual beings who also serve as divine messengers. Their very nature is all about guiding and protecting humanity and acting as a sort of intermediary between divinity and mortals. Although angels are usually associated with Christianity in the West, they don't necessarily have to be constrained to the teachings of a single religion. People from all religious backgrounds and even those who don't practice any faith can have a sense of something greater that exists above them and everyone else. Such people will also have a natural desire to get closer to that divinity, and that's where angels of all sorts come in.

Guardian angels and archangels, particularly the difference between the two, were already briefly discussed earlier in this book. Archangels, with their established and quite famous identities, have ubiquitous roles as sources of strength and inspiration for all of humanity. On the other hand, guardian angels cherish a more personal relationship with their humans, allowing for a lot more back-and-forth. This makes these angelic beings especially interesting in terms of spiritual communication.

The support you can get from your guardian angels is personalized and communicated through a lot of the usual spirit guide channels, such as dreams and synchronicities. A guardian angel might make his presence known when you're feeling discouraged and struggling with life's challenges. Apart from intuitively nudging you in the right direction or issuing warnings, guardian angels also provide an uplifting presence that can elevate your spirits and motivation. They're known to improve people's moods and promote optimism, which can be essential in keeping you on the right track.

Because of their connection with the divine and their residence in a much higher spiritual realm, angels can offer a unique perspective on problems and make you see things in a whole new light. Angels will also facilitate emotional, spiritual, and even physical healing in those who are struggling. Their presence is highly comforting and can help you overcome trauma and pain, similar to other spirit guides known for their supportive nature.

Your relationship with a guardian angel can be seen as an agreement or covenant that begins even before you are born into the physical world. Something else that sets guardian angels apart from other spirit guides is their detailed insight into your mind and soul, particularly your true goals and dreams. They understand your purpose and have access to information that's stored deeply in your heart. This profound personal understanding is why guardian angels are so supportive and encouraging.

Archangels can offer similar kinds of support, except with less of a personal touch. Archangels bring to the table a set of powerful spiritual associations and connotations, however, wielding immense divine power and possessing the ability to significantly affect the physical world. The most famous archangels include Raphael, Gabriel, Michael, and Uriel, among a few others. Respectively, they're represented by the colors yellow, blue, red, and green. In some traditions, these four archangels are also associated with the elements of air, water, fire, and earth, in the above order. In religious depictions, the archangels usually feature powerful tools or divine weapons that are specific to them, such as Michael's mighty sword, with which he slashes at injustice and malice.

Archangels also have certain specialties and roles, with Michael being known as a protector and a symbol of courage and divine truth. As such, Michael can protect you when you're feeling weak or offer guidance when you're lost. Raphael is a healer with an ability to inspire emotional and physical recovery in the afflicted. Gabriel is known as a communicative archangel who maintains a stable line with the divine and is usually called upon to facilitate communication with higher realms. Uriel is connected with the wilderness and its animals, guiding those who call upon him to a stronger connection with nature.

While communicating with a guardian angel is all about cherishing an existing relationship and strengthening your bond, archangels are usually directly invoked by name. This is done through rituals, prayer, meditation, and other methods, in addition to detecting and reading angelic signs that you might encounter in the world or in your mind and intuition. Your guardian angel is yours alone and will have a tailored approach to supporting you, while archangels are omnipresent and involved with all of humanity.

Common Angelic Signs

If you were born in a Christian cultural space, then you are probably very familiar with the concept of angels. Their role in the Christian religion has been intricately developed, and practicing the faith is, in many ways, an exercise in communicating with angels, especially archangels. Nonetheless, angelic entities should be seen as separate from individual religious dogmas, as their presence is universal and open to people from all backgrounds.

Before you learn about a few practical steps to increase your chances of receiving angelic messages, it's important to understand the wide range of signs that might signify their presence. Whatever kind of angelic entity you're interacting with, their presence can be felt or noticed through a variety of sensations or visual clues. Like a lot of other spirit guides, angels might announce their presence through scents, especially pleasant ones that smell sweet. Pay special attention to pleasant scents that emerge spontaneously without a clear source in your physical environment. For instance, a sudden scent of flowers is a common sign of angelic presence.

Because they often feature wings, angels might hint at their presence by leaving feathers in their wake. These can show up in various colors and sizes, especially in uncharacteristic places where birds don't usually visit. The more abnormal the place, the higher the likelihood is that there is an angel in your proximity. White feathers are the most frequently associated with angelic beings, although your personal guardian angel might sport a different color.

Angels are also known to communicate through numbers, especially repetitive and consecutive numbers that feel intuitively meaningful, such as 333, 777, 999, or a series of identical digits on a clock. If these numbers show up in your visual range at opportune times or recurrently, there is a good chance that an angel might be trying to draw your attention and tell you something. Angel numbers don't always have to be a succession of identical digits, however, and can include specific numbers that are personally meaningful to you, such as your birthday or that of a loved one.

Angel numbers.[17]

There is a variety of interpretations of what various three-digit sequences of angelic numbers or peculiar clock digits might mean. You can try using established interpretations, but keep in mind that angels might not speak to every person in the same way. You are more likely to derive meaning from these numbers if you closely examine the context in which you see them, including location, synchronicities, your emotional state, and your present goals. For example, seeing 11:11 on a clock is often taken as a call from the spiritual realm, urging you to listen more attentively to spirit guides and focus on the big picture in your life. 12:12 is another essential clock number to watch out for, as it implies that you should tread beyond your comfort zone to achieve your goals. The three-digit sequences are usually interpreted to contain the following messages:

- **000** – Energy can affect outcomes in a lot that you do. This is why it's important to stay positive and goal-oriented instead of getting caught up on negativity from yourself or others.
- **111** – Your thoughts require your attention because of the profound ways in which they can impact your reality and determine outcomes.
- **222** – You are following the proper path toward your goals and should stay focused.
- **333** – This number is usually taken as a reminder that the angels, divinity, and other spirits are around you, guiding you along your path.
- **444** – A common sign of angelic presence, especially regarding your guardian angels who are giving you guidance.
- **555** – Symbolizes a wind of change in your life, according to divine will, but as a reminder that you should stay the course and not become complacent.
- **666** – Despite its bad rep, the number 666 is often an angelic sign carrying positive affirmations. It serves as a reminder that you must address your spiritual needs and strive for balance.
- **777** – A powerful numerical symbol confirming that you are following the right path and are striving decisively toward your goals and in accordance with divine will.
- **888** – Similarly to 555, this number symbolizes changes while also reminding you that you should embrace these shifts and seize the opportunities that they present.
- **999** – Referring to important changes in a broader sense, the number 999 reminds you of the changes within yourself, in addition to those around you. It implies that these changes should be welcomed and used to their full potential.

Stumbling upon a random coin can also signify an angelic presence in your life. Particularly important are any inscriptions, dates, and other details that the coin might contain, which can hold messages that only you can decipher within a specific personal context. You should also pay attention to sparks and other phenomena associated with light, especially during a ritual or meditation session. Tingling in the area of your crown chakra, temperature changes, warmth, tactile sensations, sudden joy, a pleasant breeze, reassuring voices, music, and much more can also imply the presence of an angel. Angels will also willingly use popular symbols regardless of what they actually look like, simply because these symbols are widely understood by people. Be on the lookout for angelic figures with wings, trumpets, swords, doves, chalices, or angelic wings.

Feeling the Angelic Touch

Since angelic spiritual entities are classified into different categories, communicating with them boils down to a set of various exercises, as well as goals for those exercises. Your journey toward forming a close relationship with the angels will also depend on your personal needs and circumstances. It might revolve around simply locating and reading their signs, but it can also rest on prayer, meditation, and simple spiritual bonding. The overarching goal is to become more sensitive to the angels and feel their presence in your life as clearly as possible. The exercises, rituals, and tips described below will offer a variety of avenues that you can take toward that end.

Connecting with Your Guardian Angel

Unlike some other spirit guides – such as those who emerge through animals – guardian angels will rarely show up in a form that you can observe with your eyes. Therefore, it's left to the eye of your mind, your intuition, and the power of your visualization to connect with your guardian angel if you want a face-to-face interaction. As with other spirit guides, however, the most important aspect of the connection will be in the things you intuitively feel and understand, so if you struggle with visualizing your guardian angel, you shouldn't give up.

Find or create a comfortable, soothing place that you can turn into your sacred space for meditating on your angelic connections. Try to make the spot personalized and symbolic with props and decorations. Lighting can also be very important when trying to communicate with angels, with soft, dim, soothing light being especially conducive to such communication. Fill your sacred space with pleasant scents as well, such as those of lavender or via smudging. The basis of the meditation will be similar to other such rituals discussed in the book thus far.

You can visualize a journey to a magical meeting place or envision a visitation from your guardian angel as he or she descends down to you and accompanies you in your meditation. Reflect on your soul's eternal bond with this guardian angel who has accompanied you since before birth and has faithfully observed all your trials and tribulations in life but also all your joyous moments. Try to mentally capture the entirety of what this long, personal relationship means, and you'll find it easier to achieve a sense of presence at any given moment. Using affirmations filled with gratitude can also be of great help.

Archangel Invocation Ritual

To invoke the archangels essentially means to summon them and call them into your presence. The simplest, traditional way of doing this is through prayer and religious worship. It can also be done through elaborate esoteric rituals with a pentagram or hexagram, conducted at an advanced altar that features four cardinal points, the elements, proper positioning, and much more. However, you don't have to be a master of esotericism to invoke an archangel and seek his guidance, and a lot of regular people do this every day with the four primary archangels.

You can also invoke angels through esoteric rituals with a pentagram.[18]

A simple invocation ritual rests upon intention, intuition, and powerful visualization. Begin with self-reassurance that the archangels are nearby and are ready to offer their guidance. First, turn east in the usual direction of Raphael and invoke him with a simple yet firm statement such as, "To my east, emerge Raphael." Use elements of Raphael's usual depictions to reinforce the visualization, such as his yellow robe, a powerful caduceus or staff in his hand, and the element of air. You can imagine him as a man-like figure with wings or as an incarnation of energy, as long as the shape and form are agreeable to your visualization skills.

For each of the other archangels, prepare a simple statement of invocation and say it aloud as you did with Raphael. As you continue facing east in your position, invoke Michael on your right-hand side, Gabriel behind you, and Uriel on your left. Remember their respective colors, and imagine each of them in connection with their respective tools and weapons, which include Michael's mighty sword, Gabriel's chalice, and Uriel's sheaf of wheat. Don't forget the elements they're associated with as well.

Visualizing all four of the archangels and convincing yourself that they're standing around you is a major exercise in visualization, which can take a lot of time and effort. Experiment with your setting, intentions, props, and altars as much as you need to until you create your perfect space that will facilitate such rituals. Once you're confident that you're visualizing the archangels, you can also use further verbal affirmations to address them directly after assembly.

Your intention and your reasons for invoking the archangels will depend on your needs as well, so if all you need is protection, then you can focus on invoking Michael alone. If you choose to use an altar, remember to set it facing east and assign four cardinal points for each archangel in the four corners of the altar. Every cardinal point should also feature an elemental symbol, and your invocation rituals will benefit from prayers and the ritualistic use of candles. Every archangel can also have their individual candle in their respective color.

Journaling Angel Signs

The signs discussed earlier can show up seemingly at random or during one of your deliberate attempts to contact the angels. Whether the sign was a response to your inquiry or a prompt from an angel trying to initiate contact has no implications as to the sign's relevance.

They're all equally important, and you should make an effort to record every association, synchronicity, or symbol, no matter how subtle or random they might seem.

Angels come in many shapes, and they're one of the most widespread kinds of spirit guides making their way around humans. Because of this ubiquitous presence and the sheer diversity of their signs, it's a good idea to have a separate ledger serving as a journal used exclusively for angelic signs.

Write what you hear and feel and draw what you see, even if you completely forget about it within the hour. You never know when you might see something else that reminds you of a sign you saw previously, and a sudden realization of clarity just clicks. Some signs will only make sense when compared to previous experiences, which will give them a full context. Your angel sign journal is something you'll continuously study and reference as you try to understand more about what archangels and guardian angels are trying to tell you.

Angel Card Reading

Angel oracle cards are another mode of communication you might consider when trying to receive hints from angels or archangels. Angel cards are rather popular, so your first step is to pick a deck that you find most appealing. This is the part where your intuition will play an essential role. Once you pick the perfect deck of angel cards, you'll be able to use them in many ways and for various questions and messages, similar to how you'd use animal oracle cards.

Your deck can be as simple as containing yes and no answers to questions, or it can be rather complex, in which case it'll likely come with some sort of manual or guidebook for detailed interpretation. In either case, the important thing is to set clear intentions and prepare the right questions before using your cards. For simple questions that are satisfied with simple answers, you can use a simple one-card spread for a quick inquiry. Shuffle your deck thoroughly and ask a question or make a request before drawing a card to receive an answer. You can ask your questions internally, but it's also a good idea to verbalize them or even use short prayers and affirmations as if you were invoking an archangel.

Apart from a three-card spread that provides an answer with bonus insights about your past and future, just like with animal cards, you can also try a five-card spread. This spread is the perfect middle ground between simple answers and complex readings, as it can provide more information and insights regarding potential paths, propositions, and tough decisions. All you have to do is ask for guidance regarding your problem, pull five cards, and arrange them in the shape of a cross with one card in the middle and the other four on each side of it.

The central card will provide the most generalized response to your inquiry. Respectively, the cards on its left and right will refer to the past as it influences the current situation and a potential future outcome, just like in a three-card spread. The cards on the bottom and top of the central card will provide insights into your reasons for asking the question and any potential changes or opportunities that might arise from your situation.

Depending on the kind of deck you acquire, your cards might also be suitable for seven-card, Celtic cross, heart-shaped spreads, and much more. You'll also find that most decks allow for a lot of experimentation so that you can adjust them to your communication rituals in a way that best suits you and your needs.

Chapter 7: Reconnecting with Departed Loved Ones and Ancestors

For a lot of people, the main interest they have in spiritual communication is the prospect of making contact with loved ones who are no longer with them. Another common hope that spiritually curious people throughout history have had is to strengthen their bond with their ancestors and heritage. As such, departed loved ones and ancestors are some of the most important spirit guides.

Both of these kinds of spirit guides can be sources of immense strength. Getting in touch with them has the potential to make an individual feel held while also providing a powerful sense of belonging. Most human civilizations have always attributed great importance to ancestors as a means of positioning the living generation within a continuum that stretches beyond a human lifetime. On the other hand, people from across the world have always had to contend with the grief of losing the people they held dear, with many different approaches to processing these feelings.

Spiritual communication allows you to communicate with departed loved ones.[19]

Whether it's about ancestors or departed loved ones, the central theme is always the human desire to converse with those who are no longer physically present. Some people want to do this as a way of strengthening their roots, while others are looking for closure after a loss, but whatever the motive might be, this kind of spiritual communication is all about spiritual balance and comfort. This chapter will teach you more about the spirit guides found in these categories while also going over a few practical exercises that will help you get in touch with those who are no longer with you.

Departed Loved Ones, Ancestors, and the Nature of Their Communication

Why connecting with ancestors and loved ones who have passed has been so important in innumerable cultures is a multifaceted question. Part of it has to do with the fact that people across time and space have always had many things in common, particularly in regard to concerns and experiences in their lives on Earth.

Existential questions, life's trials and tribulations, and spiritual exploration are universal aspects of life that all human beings share.

To tackle such challenges, especially with respect to things that are yet to come, people have always looked for help and guidance from those who have experience in these domains. As such, the experience and legacy of those who have lived out their entire lives and seen the end have always naturally come into focus.

Departed loved ones and ancestors have not only had the full experience of life, but they also share much more with their descendants than with other, more distant people. This is what makes such spirits an eternal object of fascination and searching for people in need of guidance and spiritual support.

When you need someone who's been through the same things you're currently going through and also comes from the same place or even the same home as you, your ancestors and departed loved ones will provide the strength, inspiration, and wisdom that you need.

In a spiritual sense, ancestors and loved ones are spiritual entities that dwell in the realm of spirits while still retaining an interest in communicating what wisdom and insights they can to those who've come after them and are still among the living. The spirits of some people who have passed might not always have such interests, choosing instead to focus fully on the matters of beyond. However, it's exceedingly rare that the spirit of someone you were close with will have no desire to communicate with you on at least a basic level. Sometimes, they'll merely make their presence known without saying much that's concrete, and you will find that this is enough.

The personal nature of the bond and the aforementioned common ground that you'll have with these spirit guides will make this relationship feel like a true companionship. Knowing that others have gone through the challenges that you're facing, prevailed, and are now watching over you as you move through the motions will - at the very least -make you feel less alone in any hardship. This is the essential nature of communicating with your ancestors and departed loved ones.

Apart from enriching your life with their comforting presence, these spirit guides will certainly give you intuitive nudges and subtly point you toward decisions and paths at times. To that end, they might communicate through reminders, flashbacks, and other sudden bursts of clarity that occur at opportune times. The overwhelming sense that a loved one or an ancestor is happy with the path you are taking and is proverbially smiling down upon you is an experience that many people will have in their lives. This is one of the clearest signs of a benevolent spiritual presence by an entity that knows you intimately and understands what you're going through.

Common Signs of Ancestral or Departed Presence

Keeping in touch with departed loved ones and ancestors is one of the most intuitive forms of spiritual communication. In part, this is because of the deeply personal, emotional, and spiritual threads that bind an individual to these spirits in a way that doesn't exist with most other entities. Beyond overt signs and information, to communicate with these spirit guides is to feel the warmth and comfort of their support. For many people, this relationship boils down to feeling and cherishing the sense that these spirits are present in their lives more than engaging in informational back-and-forth.

Your ancestors or loved ones who have passed can communicate with you in two main ways. Firstly, this communication might be a one-time sign, such as a single dream or vision. Having a dream about someone who has recently passed away is a common way in which this happens for many people. By visiting you in a dream shortly after their departure, a loved one might be trying to help you process the heavy emotional residue of your loss. The dream may or may not be pleasant, but this is almost always a way for a loved one to help you adjust to the new reality of living without them while giving you some initial closure. For most people, the grieving process extends well beyond a single dream, of course, but this simple visitation is an important early step.

On the other hand, these guides can also communicate with you on an ongoing basis. How frequently that communication will occur depends both on the spirit's intentions and your own efforts. If you actively cherish the connection and engage in rituals to deepen the relationship, the frequency of the messages will undoubtedly increase. Prolonged communication with a departed loved one can last throughout a period of grieving or other personal struggle, but it can also be a life-long interaction. With ancestors, the emphasis is especially strong on long-term exchanges with the spirit realm because this relationship tends to be more meditative, ritualistic, and infused into lifelong spiritual and religious practice.

The spiritual energy that comes through from your ancestors will manifest and strengthen through your efforts to explore and approximate your heritage and your place in that long chain. As such, it's a more proactive search for signs and clues that increase in frequency as your curiosity grows. Departed loved ones tend to be a lot more spontaneous and free-flowing with the messages they send. Apart from dreams, they might also manifest through scents, songs, tastes, or images that irresistibly remind you of that person.

These clues will show up as synchronicities at meaningful moments and steer your mind and feelings in certain directions via your intuition. The signs that departed loved ones will send your way can be immeasurably diverse and subject to all manner of personal variations. There is no golden universal formula in relationships this personal, so a lot of these signs will only be known and identifiable when seen by your eyes and experienced through your emotions. The important thing is to cherish the memory of the person who was close to your heart with as much detail as possible, and then it will be easy for you to notice when they are trying to communicate in ways that only you can truly understand.

Receiving Messages from Those Who Have Passed On

As in the case of angels and archangels, departed loved ones and ancestors have similarities, but they are categories with defined differences. Increasing the presence of either in your life is once again a deeply personal journey that you are encouraged to modify, adapt, and adjust so that you are meeting your specific spiritual needs as best you can. Not everyone who seeks to connect with a departed loved one will be dealing with the trauma of an unresolved loss while seeking closure and emotional catharsis.

On the contrary, people who are at perfect peace with the natural passing of someone they hold dear can have a wide range of reasons to want to explore a deeper relationship with their loved one's spirit. Keep these personal preferences and differences in mind when learning about the following exercises, as they can benefit immensely from your personal input and adjustments.

Creating a Memory Altar

A memory altar can be an incredibly powerful tool that'll help you channel energy between yourself and a departed loved one – *or even your entire ancestral lineage.* It would work similarly to any other altar dedicated to a specific kind of spirit guide and can be as simple or as complex as you want it to be. The important thing is that your memory altar features as many items associated with the people you're remembering as possible.

Consider creating a memory altar.[30]

These objects can be photographs, heirlooms, other personal items, or anything else that once belonged to a person or is a strong reminder of them. The idea is for these reminders to maintain your focus on the memories of a person while you're at the altar performing a ritual or meditating. Personal items will be the defining feature, but your altar can still feature other default characteristics of an altar, such as religious décor and things symbolizing the four elements.

Your memory altar will serve as a spiritual retreat in a quiet place and a location where you can symbolically meet your departed loved ones and ancestors. It provides a special place where you can visualize convening with these spirits, asking them questions, and seeking their guidance. It'll also be a place for honoring these people and giving offerings to them.

Ancestral Meditation

As usual, meditation will serve as one of the methods of communication with these spirit guides. If you build a memory altar, you'll have an easily accessible place for this kind of meditation in your home, filled with all sorts of props that will potentiate the flow of energies and keep your intention strong. To create a setting conducive to this kind of communication, you can also use music that the departed once enjoyed or something that's associated with your ancestors as a whole. As a general rule, meditation works best in silence, but in this case, a melody can strengthen a sense of presence and familiarity while also triggering certain emotions. As long as the music is at a low volume and is relaxing, it's something worth experimenting with.

Begin by getting into a comfortable position and a breathing exercise for relaxation. Position yourself at your memory altar or surround yourself with meaningful items that remind you of the people you are trying to communicate with. You can visualize that the departed is at your home and is present in the room with you, or you can imagine a more complex encounter scenario happening at another place, particularly a location that's attached to shared memories. You can also picture a gathering of supportive ancestors sitting around a table or, better yet, your altar. Create a meditative journey similar to how you would meet your power animal or a nature spirit and gradually work your way toward the moment when you can ask questions and seek guidance. Make sure to make a written note of any feelings and insights once you're done with your meditation.

Letter to a Departed Loved One

Sometimes, the best approach is to simply engage in direct conversation with the spirit of a departed loved one. Apart from being direct, this form of dialogue is subtle, personal, and easy to engage in wherever you find yourself. You can write this letter when you're spending time out in nature or at home. The only thing that matters are the contents of the letter, which should feature plenty of back-and-forth and treat your departed loved one as much as a living person as possible. Don't simply ask questions and make demands. Try to make it a real conversation, providing family updates, comments, and reminiscing that your loved one would be interested in.

While you can write this private letter anywhere, it matters where you place it after you're done. It should be left at a meaningful place where the presence of the departed is felt the strongest. You'll have the best idea of what place evokes these emotions in you, but some of the usual examples include the person's resting place at the cemetery, shared favorite locations, locations of important past events between you and the departed, or a memory altar. It's also a good idea to read the letter aloud at your memory altar to verbalize the message and strengthen the connection. You can keep this letter and read it as an overture to meditation and visualization, using it as a starting point that commences a conversation.

Automatic Writing

Because parts of your departed loved ones and ancestors live on inside you, you'll have a natural advantage when it comes to mediumship with these spirits. You are bound to have quite a few things in common with them in terms of your personality, mentality, and intuitive feelings. This is why automatic writing can be a very fruitful addition to your efforts of channeling messages between yourself and these spirits. As described earlier in the book, automatic writing allows you to pour out the thoughts and emotions that come to you via intuition without any filters, unclouded by analysis and second-guessing.

Refer back to the basics of automatic writing as discussed in the third chapter) and think of the best way to direct this method at your departed loved one or ancestors. The aforementioned letter, for instance, is an excellent opportunity to use automatic writing. The spirit might already be active around you and trying to communicate, so if you use automatic writing for your letter, you might find that the writing becomes a joint exercise between you and the spirit. You never know what the spirit might channel through you as you write, so it's important to spend some time analyzing the content later on. Their messages could be coded, subtle, and difficult to spot at first, being hidden in plain sight and appearing as your own words at first glance.

Dream Journaling

Every dream that references your ancestors or departed loved ones in any way will be extremely meaningful, no matter how simple or shallow it might seem at first glance. It's important to keep a clear record of these dreams, featuring as much detail as possible. Write down the details of conversations, any symbols you see, or any feelings you experience in the dream. All of these will contain essential insights that you must analyze to derive their full meaning.

Keeping a dream journal can strengthen your connection with your departed loved ones.[21]

It can also help if you practice setting intentions before going to sleep, especially during the last few minutes before you go under. Focus your mental energy and try to imagine a dream with as much detail as possible and let yourself shut down right in the middle of your thought process. Even if this doesn't produce the exact dream you were hoping for, it's very likely to make your dream more vivid and memorable. Keeping a dream journal is also known to train the brain's ability to recall dreams after waking up. This might eventually unlock lucid dreaming as well, in which you'll control the narrative and have any conversation you desire. Dreams are best remembered right after you awake, so your journal and a pen should be kept handy on your nightstand so that you can start writing first thing in the morning.

Chapter 8: Communicating with Ascended Masters

On a plane of existence much higher than that of regular humans and perhaps even that of other spirit guides, there exist figures commonly referred to as the ascended masters. According to most interpretations, these are enlightened beings that occupy a higher dimension and have transcended beyond the processes described in major religions, such as the cycle of reincarnation. Usually, they were once people who had ascended to this higher plane by elevating their consciousness and spirit.

The ascended masters are usually given a few unique properties that separate them from the spirit guides discussed thus far. They are still there to

Ascended masters are enlightened beings that occupy a higher dimension.[22]

offer guidance and wisdom to people, but their realm is on a whole other level. The ascended masters can be seen as the highest echelon of guiding spiritual entities, but that doesn't mean they are beyond reach. Their power is in the immortal example they have set for other spiritually-minded people who came after them.

Seasoned mediums or those practitioners who put enough effort and practice into spiritual communication can learn how to receive messages even from the highest order of spiritual beings. This final chapter will close off the story about spiritual communication by teaching you more about these special kinds of spirit guides. You'll also learn how you might be able to absorb some of the wisdom that they can teach if you're willing to go the extra mile.

Who Are the Ascended Masters?

Generally speaking, the ascended masters represent spiritual teachers who have elevated themselves to levels of spirituality and consciousness beyond normal human comprehension. Embodied and exemplified by spiritual giants and deities such as Christ, Gautama Buddha, Mary, Guanyin, St. Germain, and others, the ascended masters often feature rather human forms or are outright based on people who once lived.

The concept of ascended masters is a major theme in the traditions of theosophy, which is a mixture of religious practices and philosophy that originated in the 19th-century United States. Theosophy is often not proclaimed to be a religion, but at the very least, it can be seen as a philosophical and spiritual system that brings together religious and philosophical teachings from across the world. It prominently features aspects of Eastern religions like Hinduism and Buddhism, as well as ancient European philosophy. Since the early days of theosophy, the ideas surrounding the ascended masters have proliferated and been adopted into various other practices as well.

According to theosophical tradition, the ascended masters are defined by having past human incarnations. As such, they were once ordinary people who, through tremendous spiritual work and effort, were able to complete a number of transformations. These transformations, also referred to in theosophy as initiations, allowed the ascended masters to reach such a level of spiritual enlightenment that they eventually escaped the cycle of rebirth. It is the hope of those who seek to contact and follow the example of the ascended masters that they'll be able to draw at least some of that wisdom and power to be used toward their own spiritual development. This is why the ascended masters, beyond strict theosophical practice, are often regarded as another group of spirit guides.

Although these enlightened souls now dwell in realms beyond the five human senses, the mark that they left upon the world was tremendous. Their legacy is one of wisdom, passion, healing, enlightenment, and compassion. In many cases, the ascended masters helped others both spiritually and physically during their time on earth, as opposed to simply pursuing their own enlightenment.

One of the defining features of the ascended masters is their universality across different cultures. This body of teachings draws from all major religious traditions and brings them together into one comprehensive spiritual system. They bring together cultures, races, ethnicities, and religions, representing a wealth of spiritual heritage and wisdom. It's also not uncommon for some of the ascended masters to be venerated in multiple major religions – with one example being Jesus, who plays a prominent role in both Christianity and Islam.

Free from the cycle of rebirth as understood in Eastern traditions and of worldly suffering, the ascended masters have attained immortality through their spiritual perfection. Unlike guardian angels and other spiritual entities that might follow you on your path, the ascended masters can be understood as healers, prophets, and teachers, each representing a unique individual with their own characteristics.

One of the essential truths that follow from the human past behind every ascended master is that every person has the capacity to become one. Ascending to this level of spirituality and higher consciousness is an exceedingly rare, historic anomaly, of course, but it's an ideal that all spiritually curious individuals can strive toward.

The Value and Ways of Ascended Master Communication

Perhaps the greatest source of power and meaning of the ascended masters is in the shining examples that they've set for humanity. As such, these unique guides can provide people with inspiration and serve as sources of strength in your time of need. Every ascended master is also a fountain of learning, offering profound insight into life paths that lead toward spiritual actualization.

Listening to what the ascended masters can teach will guide you on a path toward self-empowerment, spiritual and emotional healing, enlightenment, and much more. While other kinds of spirit guides can offer similar guidance, the ascended masters represent unique stories of spiritual life that can teach you a lot about the often difficult yet incredibly fruitful ways of living that these historical figures once lived. Developing a close relationship with one or more of the ascended masters is akin to finding a mentor on your spiritual journey, which is a role that's markedly different from that of most other spirit guides.

Another way in which the ascended masters differ from other spirit guides is in how their presence is felt. Whereas other spirit guides might make themselves known through symbols, messages, and visions, the ascended masters are more likely to be intuitively felt. Common signs of connection with an ascended master include feelings of profound inner peace, sudden clarity regarding the right path in a difficult time in your life, and overall feelings of love and compassion.

A regular spirit guide will speak to you as directly as they can, often about a specific issue that's troubling you. They'll also spontaneously leave messages that will await your discovery and interpretation. On the other hand, communicating with the ascended masters will often be a proactive endeavor on your part. They might sometimes come into your life when they are needed, but mostly, it's up to you to seek out the guidance of the ascended masters and build your personal relationship with them.

An ascended master will communicate with you when you put in the effort to contact them because you'll feel their presence on an emotional and spiritual level. They will communicate with those individuals who follow a spiritual path toward enlightenment with tremendous dedication. An ascended master's central role is to help human beings along that path and guide them toward higher levels of consciousness, with the hope that a gifted few might ascend through their initiations and reach the same level.

That spiritual support is the primary benefit of building a connection with the ascended masters. While other spirit guides will empower you with specific insights and messages of a deeply personal nature, the ascended masters are there to imbue your spirit with strength, clarity, and inspiration. They will bring compassion and love into your life, reinforcing your sense that you aren't alone and that there's a spiritual ideal that's worth striving for.

Getting in Touch with Ascended Masters

There are many ways in which you can foster a relationship with one or more ascended masters. Since a lot of them are central figures in major religions, practicing these faiths can also be seen as a way of cherishing your relationship with an ascended master. However, mainline religions maintain interpretations that are fairly different from those found in the traditions of theosophy. As such, trying to get in touch with the ascended masters on your own can be seen as a complementary endeavor that can enhance your conventional religious practices.

Meditation, daily rituals, and other similar activities can only serve to propel you further on your path toward spiritual fulfillment, as you'll find in the instructions discussed below.

You can get in touch with ascended masters through meditation.[38]

Meeting Ascended Masters through Visualization and Meditation

Since the ascended masters are well-defined individuals with their own personalities, trying to connect with them directly will work very well as a meeting visualization. Refer back to what you've learned earlier about shamanic journeying or meeting your animal totem in an envisioned place of wonder and natural spirituality. Try to come up with a similar scenario that fits particularly well with the ascended master you're trying to visualize. Think of creating a story such as a meeting with Christ in

Nazareth or a walk along the Ganges in ancient India with Siddhartha before he attained Buddhahood.

Imagine a peaceful plane in a higher-dimensional space where insightful meetings can occur between the curious souls of mortals and those of the ascended masters. Set your intention toward a particular ascended master, a place, and a question before you begin your meditation. Focus your mind's eye upward toward a plane of existence that exists as physically higher than the observable world of humans. Follow a visualized stairway upward as it's conjured up from white light or the moonlight on a clear night.

Whatever kind of place you picture in your mind and whatever way you imagine will lead you there, focus on the ascended master and all of his unique characteristics. Famous and legendary figures have a whole lot that defines them, so it should be easier to imagine them as real beings with faces and traits. This is why it's important to understand the ascended masters who pique your interest and study them a fair amount before thinking you are ready to meet them. When the interaction finally comes, make sure that you know what you want to ask and are prepared to receive the answers.

Daily Wisdom Practice

Your relationship with the ascended masters is something that you can work on every day. There are many ascended masters residing on those higher planes of existence beyond the ones briefly mentioned earlier. Practicing the wisdom of the ascended masters on a daily basis can work as a daily meditation plan in which every day of the week is dedicated to a particular master. You can start the week by meditating upon the life and works of Christ on Monday, and Siddhartha Gautama on Tuesday, before taking a stroll into ancient Chinese spirituality or Hinduism on the following day.

How you practice wisdom and interact with the ascended masters on a daily basis is entirely up to you. The only true rule that you must heed is the necessity of studying these figures and their legacy as much as you have the time for. For instance, a simple yet potentially profound way to start your morning is to find a quote by a particular ascended master and spend some time reflecting on what it means. Many of the ascended masters have left behind a wealth of earthly wisdom, which is studied by billions of people to this day.

Their quotes and tidbits of their expansive minds often hold a lot more meaning than is immediately apparent. If you spend at least fifteen minutes during your morning routine analyzing such thoughts and meditating on their meaning, you might eventually discover that you're starting to look at certain things in a new light. Every time you meditate upon one of the masters, remember that the main goal is to bring at least a bit of influence and inspiration from them into your life. You must set clear intentions toward that end, with an understanding that their presence alone can give you an immense spiritual boost even if you don't engage in any concrete back-and-forth.

Sacred Reading and Reflection

In a way, you can choose your preferred ascended master and develop your bond with them similarly to how you would with your animal totem. This similarity concerns the part of animal totem bonding that has to do with studying the animal you feel drawn toward.

Remember: many of the ascended masters used to be humans who achieved their high status through intense spiritual work, thus leaving a mark on major world religions. These faiths all feature an immense body of scripture, sacred texts, and endless other material that you can study. Studying these texts or just learning about the stories from an ascended master's mortal life are both great ways of making yourself feel closer to such figures.

Your first impression might be that it's going to be difficult to relate to the struggles of people who lived 2,000 years ago or even earlier. Once you start reading, however, you'll find that there is a whole lot about the human experience that hasn't really changed on a fundamental level. This is especially true of spiritual pursuits and existential questions, which remain as relevant as ever and essentially the same. Some of the Hindu Vedas, for example, go back more than 3,000 years, and having such direct insight into the spirituality of those days can be a fascinating experience.

It's important that you never read these sacred texts merely as a way to kill time or as a fashion statement. These writings demand attention and should be read mindfully, regardless of your cultural background or personal beliefs. If you truly commit to studying sacred texts and scripture, it's a good idea to start a separate journal where you can make quick notes of your observations, interpretations, and feelings about the things you read.

Appendix: Spirit Messages – Common Signs and Symbols

Now that you understand how spiritual communication works and what the usual sources of these messages are, it's up to you to come up with routines and ritual combinations that best fit into your lifestyle and interests. Keep in mind that honing your intuition and becoming more present and aware in your daily life is the key to noticing spirit messages.

To round things off, this appendix will provide a small but handy glossary of common messages, signs, and symbols that you're likely to encounter when searching for communications from your spirit guides. The appendix will also serve as a partial recap by summarizing some of the messages already discussed in the previous chapters and combining them with a few that weren't mentioned. Having all of these listed out and briefly summarized in one place will hopefully allow you to keep the list close at hand for quick reference both in your daily life and your rituals.

Animals

Since animals can be such important conduits of spiritual communication, they deserve special attention. Be on the lookout for any animals that you feel a special connection to, and take note of their powerful symbolism that can be found in almost all spiritual traditions in history. When an animal crosses your path, pay heed to how it behaves, what it does, and where the encounter occurred. If a wild animal stops to look at you and gives you attention, especially in a natural setting, you might be witnessing a powerful sign.

Birds

While birds fall under the broader category of animals, some species are particularly noteworthy. Refer to earlier parts in this book that mention many important symbols associated with animals, which have cropped up in many of the world's religions. The behavior of birds can be especially meaningful, particularly if they land on or near you and display an uncharacteristic inclination toward interacting with you.

Butterflies

Butterflies are a common symbol of transformation, owing to the natural way in which they develop and enter the world. Some traditions consider them to symbolize benevolent souls coming to visit you. Turn to your introspection and intuition, paying attention to the person or memory that seems to come to your mind most frequently when you encounter a butterfly. As such, a butterfly can represent the fact that a departed loved one has successfully made it over to the other side or is sending you a message of love and support.

Celestial Bodies

The stars, moon, and sun can all carry important messages if you know what to look for. Noticing patterns in the night sky or around the rising or setting sun as it casts its light through the clouds around it can convey meaning depending on how you're feeling or what you're thinking at that moment. The same holds true for the moon and its many shapes, locations, and colors, ranging from red to silver.

Clock Signs

Clocks, and time in general, can sometimes elicit strange feelings, especially when your mind starts noticing patterns and synchronicities. If you observe a perfect set of identical numbers, such as 22:22 or 11:11, or a symmetrical instance like 13:13, it could be a message from a spiritual source. Perhaps a person you hold dear is thinking of you, or it could be a departed loved one or another form of spirit guide. In a time of struggle, this realization can offer reassurance and support. At times of happiness or success, it could mean that someone who passed away is looking over you and sharing in your joy.

Cloud Patterns and Shapes

Similarly to celestial bodies, clouds should be observed whenever you have the opportunity to spend some time in reflection and introspection. Look for patterns and shapes that might materialize as the clouds slowly rumble along their way across the sky, and you might be surprised by what you find. Due to their immense variability in size and shape (and their constant shifting), clouds usually abound in meaning and are a common channel that spiritual entities use to communicate. Reading into clouds can also have therapeutic effects and can be incorporated into various meditative exercises.

Coins

A coin is another one of those ubiquitous small objects that can show up in odd places and at peculiar times. It's not merely due to their association with money and wealth that coins have often been associated with luck when found lying around. If you run into a coin when you least expect it, you should take note of the situation in which you found it and look at potential synchronicities. Inspect such a coin closely, and you might be surprised by the numbers or words on it and how they might relate to your latest thoughts, intentions, or actions.

Displacement of Objects

As you've learned, various inanimate objects can serve as conduits of spiritual messages. In particular, if you find that certain items disappear, move, or reappear inexplicably, it could be a spiritual entity's way of trying to communicate. You should be mindful of how some objects – particularly ones that you thought you had lost – reappear at times and places that seem oddly coincidental. An object might reappear exactly when you need it, which is clear enough, but it might also show up only for you to then realize that you need it.

Feathers

While feathers were discussed earlier as one of the common signs of spiritual communication, it's also worth noting that they are widespread in the physical world. Not every feather will carry a special meaning or message for you, especially if you can find a clear, logical explanation for its presence at a certain place. As always, look for synchronicities and try to determine if a feather has shown up within a meaningful concept. Finding a feather next to a bird nest and having one flutter on a dash of wind through your window and land directly on you are two very different scenarios.

General Repetition

Repetition and patterns, in the broadest sense, are major signs of spiritual messaging reaching you from beyond. Pattern recognition is an innate human ability, so don't let yourself succumb to confirmation bias, but also keep in mind that certain things will undoubtedly repeat and reoccur for a reason. If you notice certain colors, numbers, or codes consistently showing up, especially within a context that also seems to repeat itself, it's a good idea to give it more thought and analysis.

Light Disturbances

The flickering of lights or similar malfunctions is often misconstrued as a sign of paranormal activity, but this is a pop-culture misconception. Remember what you learned about energy and the important role it plays in the universe, your life, and all things spiritual. All of the spiritual entities you might be communicating with can, in essence, be seen as forms of energy, not too different from electricity. If a light flickers and signifies a spiritual presence, this will be a time for listening and observing, not worrying.

Moments of Clarity

Having a moment of clarity is not an uncommon consequence of spiritual intervention. It can be a spirit guide's way of telling you that you have reached an important realization or are about to uncover a great truth that will have a significant effect on your life. If you find yourself arriving at an important conclusion suddenly and without a clear, logical path in your thinking, you can be fairly certain that this important information was communicated to you by an overseeing spiritual force.

Music

As an essential aspect of the human experience, music carries a lot of meaning and energy, operating on various frequencies. The human mind has a special keenness for music and has a way of attaching memories, experiences, places, people, and much more to specific songs. As such, music lends itself to all manner of synchronicities that can make you feel and remember many things. Look for coincidences, such as a certain song coming on at a special moment that relates to it in your memories and thoughts. For instance, thinking of a departed loved one while switching on the radio, only to find that it's playing their favorite song, is a powerful message.

Orbs

Orbs, particularly those showing up in photographs, look like light balls that hover around people, objects, and spaces in some photos. Mediums commonly interpret these as signs of a spiritual presence. They usually don't carry a lot of specific meaning and are instead just a way for spirit guides to make their presence known. Still, the meaning of these orbs can vary depending on the context. If your photograph depicts an important event in your life, such as a wedding, then the presence of benevolent spiritual entities can serve as a source of reassurance.

Recurrent Waking

Waking too often in the middle of the night is usually a sign of sleep problems, but if it takes on a strange pattern, it might be much more meaningful and positive than a health issue. If, for instance, you find yourself frequently waking up at the same time, it may well be an attempt by a spiritual entity to bring your attention to something. Such a pattern of waking might also be accompanied by a recurrent thought or feeling that always follows, all of which can have a personal meaning for you.

Scents

Your sense of smell can uncover a strange presence, send you on a rollercoaster of memories, or provoke any number of intense reactions. Thanks to relational memory, certain smells can become attached to past events, feelings, and especially people. Many people have had the peculiar experience of noticing a smell that seems identical to that of a person they know well. If that person happens to be a departed loved one, noticing such a smell can be a powerful experience that reinforces their presence in spirit.

Sensations

Physical sensations can mean a lot of different things, but it's not uncommon for them to be caused by spiritual messages. The idea of being "touched" frequently appears in discussions of spiritual experiences because of this. Tactile feelings that have no clear origin in anything physical and when no contact is made with a person or object can be a strong indication of a spiritual presence. If you happen upon such an experience, take note of the context in which it occurs. If it coincides with a spiritual communication ritual or thoughts of a departed loved one, any physical sensation can become one of the most powerful spiritual messages you'll ever experience.

Sounds

With regard to spiritual communication, sounds work very similarly to scents and other physical stimuli. The sharpness of individual senses will vary from person to person, so you might garner more meaning from sounds than from scents or tactile sensations. However, keep in mind that the soundscape of the modern world is cluttered with endless interference, so your hearing is more likely to deceive you than most other senses. It's always important to use logic and try to eliminate any worldly explanations before concluding that a spiritual presence is at play. As a channel of spiritual communication, sound will probably work best in the quiet of your meditative space or out in nature, far from the buzzing of urban life.

Sudden Peace

Sudden and pleasantly overwhelming feelings of peace and balance are frequently signs of a benevolent spiritual presence. If you find yourself feeling content, peaceful, and balanced for no discernable reason, it's likely that some kind of spiritual entity is channeling its support to you or is trying to signal that you are on the right path. It can also signify some important breakthrough or spiritual milestone where you or someone you held dear has turned an important corner.

Synchronicities

As you've learned, synchronicities are very important in the world of spirituality. They are a broad yet incredibly consequential category of signs that serve as one of the major avenues of communication for spiritual entities. These entities cannot converse with you clearly and in person, so they will try to get important points across to you via apparent coincidences of all sorts. It's not an accident that the human mind is so sensitive to noticing synchronicities, which makes them difficult to miss. That's why synchronicities are a perfect tool for spiritual entities who want to get your attention. As always, your analyses and interpretations of these signs will unlock the hidden meaning behind them. Pay close attention to those synchronicities that seem to align perfectly with what you're thinking, intending, or doing at a given time, as this can be a clear sign that you are on a good course.

Temperature Changes

Like sounds and fragrances, peculiar shifts in temperature are a solid indication of some sort of presence. As always, don't interpret this as a sign of paranormal activity or anything else that you might consider menacing. As discussed, spirit guides will rarely, if ever, materialize in a physical form, but their energies can sometimes be so intense that they leave physical albeit subtle trails in the world. This is especially true if a strange temperature change occurs indoors where the effects of weather will be minimal and certainly insufficient to dramatically alter the ambient temperature at a moment's notice.

Thoughts

Your thoughts are an area worthy of exploration when it comes to identifying spiritual messages. As much as you might have control over your thoughts from a rational point of view, it's sometimes difficult to be sure about the exact seed from which a certain thought has sprouted. Most of all, it's a good idea to try and analyze the patterns you might observe in your thinking. Doing this without biases and subjectivity is easier said than done, so a journal can be of great help. You should pay particular attention to any recurrent thoughts that seem to come back frequently or any thought loops you often find yourself in.

Visions in Dreams

As you've learned, dreams play a major role in spiritual communication because they provide a canvas for all manner of spiritual messaging. Dream journaling and interpretation are all but essential if you are to unlock the true meaning behind the messages you receive from the spiritual realm. Visible symbols, people, and other living creatures are especially noteworthy motifs to analyze and interpret with regard to messages, although most other aspects of dreams can also be important for other purposes.

Visions in General

Any kind of waking vision, whether subtle or overt, is very likely to be a spirit message. Visions often come from your subconscious mind, but keep in mind that spiritual communication relies heavily on intuition. A vision coming from within doesn't mean that it's not being facilitated by an outside energy or spiritual presence. Visions can be enlightening experiences that reveal important truths and answers in your life, so they should always be analyzed and, ideally, recorded in some form.

Conclusion

The point to really take home is that spirit guides aren't there to take command or appear before you and tell you what you should do with your life. You must understand that spiritual communication shouldn't even be seen as a form of direct conversation in any sense. While spirit guides are certainly entities that operate outside of you, communicating with them actually boils down to looking deep into yourself. Their messages are there to help those who are already on a spiritual path, and the answers contained in those messages will emerge in a person's mind and heart. This means that despite the fact that the messages come from outside, they are read by looking inward.

The same holds true even for those signs and messages that you can directly see, whether they come through animals or inanimate objects in the physical world. These things are there for you to observe, but interpreting them can only be done through introspection and via your own intuition. It might be a strange concept to wrap your head around at first, but once you stop anthropomorphizing the spirit guides, it will quickly dawn on you.

This book has taught you about the different forms of spirit guides, how they operate, and how you can become more mindful of their messages directed at you and all of humanity. Beyond that, you'll have to explore the recesses of your own spirit, mind, and life if you are to get the most out of spiritual communication. With enough reflection and spiritual effort on your part, you will find that a moderate amount of spiritual guidance and a slight nudge in the right direction was all you ever needed in the first place. The knowledge that there are benevolent spirits hovering around you and other people at all times will further reassure you and inspire confidence in your ability to get over grief, find peace, prosper, and place your feet firmly on the right path.

Part 2: Manifestation

Unlock the Power of Manifesting Your Dreams through Secret Formulas, Quantum Jumping, Visualizations, 369, Affirmations, and More

Introduction

Being wealthy, lasting love, and the rekindling of relationships are among the most common themes of manifestation, but most people have doubts about how to achieve them. Manifestation is very tricky to work with. In essence, it is the practice of transmitting your thoughts and ideas into reality. It involves setting more pronounced intentions and accompanying them with clear visualizations of your goal. Most people think that manifestation is magic and that they'll wake up to find that their visualizations have come to life.

However, if you work a minimum wage job, you won't become a millionaire overnight, even if you have manifested and clearly visualized this desire. Manifestation will keep you focused on your goals, open new doors, reduce the roadblocks you encounter, and direct you toward the right opportunities and people. It's up to you to stay determined, build discipline, take actionable steps, and make the most out of the tools, people, and opportunities that come your way.

As you manifest and visualize your desires, work on building skills like self-confidence, self-control, and determination. When you add effort to your intention, you will likely achieve better results. Manifestation also requires you to take control of your thoughts and feelings and do your best to keep a positive mindset. It helps to break down your goals, determine your actions to get there, and trust that opportunities will start popping up out of nowhere.

Serving as a comprehensive guide to effective manifestation techniques, this is the only book about manifestation you'll ever have to read. In this book, you will find many practical activities and exercises backed by indispensable knowledge and guidance. By the end of this book, you'll have mastered the art of spiritual and psychic communication.

This book will guide you through the core principles of manifestation as it delves into the mechanics of how your thoughts and intentions can be transmitted into reality. You'll learn how to build a strong, positive mindset for manifestation. Then, you will understand how effective visualization can activate your subconscious mind and align your energy with your intentions, and you will learn about vivid visualization techniques.

In this book, you'll also learn about the power of affirmations and understand how you can come up with your own positive statements that you can relate to. You'll learn about the 369 Method, among the most popular and effective manifestation techniques, and other secret manifestation formulas. This book will also introduce you to the concept of quantum jumping and reality shifting, well-versing you on how you can jump into alternate realities or futures to align with your desires. Finally, you'll discover how to incorporate manifestation practices into your daily routine.

Chapter 1: Decoding Manifestation Basics

Close your eyes and envision that you have the power to achieve your goals. Imagine that anything you visualize can become a reality. This isn't magic. It's manifestation. While working hard is crucial to accomplish your dreams, you must also align your thoughts, feelings, beliefs, and actions with your goals. You may struggle if you don't believe in yourself or allow your negative thoughts to make you focus on challenges instead of opportunities.

Manifestation basics are the foundation of your journey to enlightenment.[34]

Manifestation isn't just wishing for something and waiting for it to come true. It is a process that requires taking specific steps that bring you closer to your goal and understanding the impact of your thoughts and intentions on your reality. Manifestation is a great skill that can take you far in life.

This chapter explains concepts such as manifestation, the law of attraction, universal energy, the quantum universe, and the multiverse concept. It also explores the roles of vibration and frequency. You will also discover manifestation formulas and frameworks, the science behind them, the power of belief, and emotional alignment.

Defining Manifestation

The word manifestation means transforming an idea into reality. Manifestation is defined as materializing your desires by aligning your thoughts, feelings, beliefs, and actions with your goals. It is a self-development technique that involves setting intention, repeating positive affirmations, and practicing visualizations. Social psychologist Dr Kinga Mnich describes it as "A holistic approach that brings your desires to life by living your dreams." Therapist Elizabeth Winkler describes it as a creation process that involves self-reflection and discovering the life of your dreams and what you need to do to manifest it.

Manifestation connects the body, mind, and spirit and aligns your energy with the universe. It focuses on releasing negative emotions and thoughts, limiting beliefs, and replacing them with positivity. It requires recognizing one's goals, envisioning success, focusing on the positive, and practicing gratitude to transform your intentions into tangible reality. It is based on the belief that focusing on your desires motivates you to take action and achieve your goals.

Manifestation is more effective when you act like you have already achieved your goals. For instance, if you want to get promoted at work, you should prepare yourself by dressing more professionally, adopting the mindset and habits associated with the new role, and socializing with people holding similar positions. This will show you how it feels to have your goal manifested, motivating you to work hard to achieve it.

Some people argue that manifestation isn't practical. They think it only involves setting intentions and visualization. However, it is a complex process that requires choosing reasonable goals and realistic strategies to focus one's attention and energy on manifesting one's desires.

People who use manifestation understand the significance of the mind in this process. It can transform negative thoughts by influencing the subconscious to think positively. Hence, you start believing in your abilities and chances of success.

Manifestation can be summed up in four words, "ask, believe, and receive." Simply ask the universe for what you want, believe that you have already received it, and you will receive it.

Law of Attraction and Universal Energy

The law of attraction is one of the 12 universal laws, and it suggests that positive energy attracts positive outcomes while negative energy attracts negative outcomes. You can attract anything you want by aligning your energy with the universe. Alignment is matching your energy or vibrational frequency with what you want. It's feeling happy and confident because you are certain that everything you want is coming to you. You aren't worried about how your dreams will manifest. You surrender to the universe and trust its wisdom.

The Law of Attraction's Main Principles

- **Focusing on the Present:** The law of attraction suggests that everyone has the power to improve or alter their present. Most people work hard to have a better future. They believe they can't do anything to change their current circumstances and focus their attention on the future. However, the law indicates that while the present can be flawed, you shouldn't give in or live unhappily. The past is behind you, and the future isn't guaranteed. The present is all you have. So you should use all your effort and energy to make this moment the best it can be.

- **Making Space for Positive Energy:** Releasing negative energy and thoughts makes space for positivity. The law of attraction suggests that the mind is always full, and another must always take its place when you remove something. You should always let go of what doesn't serve you and replace it with what benefits you.

- **Similar Things Attract Each Other:** You attract people, thoughts, and energies similar to you. Negative thoughts can bring negativity to every aspect of your life, while positive thinking can attract positive experiences that can transform your life.

The Law of Attraction Sub-Laws

The law of attraction consists of seven sub-laws.

1. **Manifestation:** This law suggests that you can improve your present by focusing your energy on changing yourself and your life. Obsessing over past mistakes and worrying about the future will not change your life or help you move forward. Working on improving the present is the only way to make peace with the past and prepare for the future.
2. **Harmony:** The harmony and balance in your environment impact your energy. You should tap into this energy to create a positive mindset while working on your goals. You should also surround yourself with like-minded people who inspire, support, and encourage you to accomplish your goals.
3. **Magnetism:** People attract what they think. If you focus on the positive, your perspective will change. You will start seeing an opportunity in every challenge, which will improve your mood and well-being.
4. **Universal Influence:** This is the most important law of attraction principle. It is similar to Newton's third law, " For every action (force) in nature, there is an equal and opposite reaction." What you send out to the world comes back to you. This doesn't only apply to thoughts and emotions but also to behavior. For instance, if you disrespect a coworker, they will treat you the same. If you work hard, you will reap the benefit of your effort. If you are a good person, you will be able to help others and make a difference in the world. As a result, you will influence the universe, and the world will be a better place.
5. **Unwavering Desires**: This law suggests that people should focus on the goals that align with their plans, such as strengthening their relationships, advancing their careers, or exercising to improve their health. You should be aware of your desires and understand that your goals can change at any stage of your life. However, if you know who you are and trust your abilities, you can achieve all your goals.
6. **Delicate Balance:** While some days are good, others can be bad. You may face obstacles, experience failure, or heartbreak. You need to accept that setbacks are a part of life. Celebrate your wins, embrace your losses, and learn from your mistakes.

7. **Right Action:** You may experience situations that can make life challenging, such as an unsatisfying career or a toxic relationship. You may believe there is no way out, and you will be stuck in these situations for the rest of your life. However, this law suggests that you have the power to let go of all the things that hold you back and replace them with your purpose and the skills you need to achieve your goals.

The Role of Frequency and Vibration

The law of attraction suggests that everything and everyone is made of energy operating at different frequencies. To manifest your goals, change the frequency of negative energy with positive energy and thoughts. Use gratitude to recognize all the blessings the universe has bestowed on you. Focus on achieving your goals instead of worrying about failure.

Humans, all other living creatures, and objects are made of cells. Their frequency reflects the speed of these cells' vibrational patterns. Fast or high vibrations mean high energy and frequency, while slow or low vibration means low energy and frequency.

Each person vibrates at a subtle and different frequency. If you are sad or sick, you will vibrate at a lower frequency, while if you are healthy and happy, you will vibrate at a higher frequency.

According to renowned researcher Dr. David R. Hawkins, emotions generate an energy field. He recognized that negative emotions such as hatred, fear, and anger have low frequencies. In contrast, positive emotions such as gratitude, joy, and love have high frequencies.

Similarly, thoughts vibrate at different frequencies. The universe can identify the unique vibrations your thoughts release. For instance, you will never advance in your career if you constantly think you aren't good enough to get promoted. These negative thoughts are released to the universe in the form of frequencies and manifest and become a reality. Although this may seem disconcerting, you can use this information to your advantage.

You should pay attention to the frequencies and vibrations you emit because you will attract situations, experiences, and people that vibrate at a similar frequency. If you train your brain to think positively, you will raise your thought frequencies and manifest what you desire.

You are what you think, and emotions are the by-product of your thoughts. You can experience positive or negative feelings depending on the frequency of these emotions.

Intentions also carry unique frequencies and are extremely powerful – which is exactly why one should set an intention before manifestation to send positive vibrations to the universe and attract what one desires.

Manifestation Formulas and Frameworks

You probably wonder how manifestation works. Do you close your eyes and make a wish? Do you write it down? Manifestation is a process that involves structured formulas and approaches that can help you make your dreams a reality. Manifestation formulas are practical methods that allow you to focus your intentions and energy toward specific goals.

The 369 Manifestation Method

Renowned engineer and inventor Nikola Tesla believed that the numbers three, six, and nine are powerful and hold the keys to understanding the universe. Manifesting with these numbers aligns your goals with the universe, allowing you to tap into its energy and bring your dreams to life.

Nikola Tesla believed that the numbers three, six, and nine are powerful.[35]

The 369 manifestation method is a simple technique that involves repeating affirmations that align with your desires three times in the morning, six times in the afternoon, and nine times before bed.

The key to this method is consistency. You can't practice the 369 method once a week or whenever you remember it. It should be a part of your daily routine, and you should practice it until your desires are manifested. Consistency is necessary to keep your mind and energy focused on achieving your goals.

Scripting

Scripting is another manifestation approach that allows you to focus your intentions and energy on specific goals. It is a creative process that involves writing down your goals as if you are already living them. You should picture your life if your desires were manifested and describe every detail, thought, and emotion. Make it as vivid as possible. This technique is based on the law of attraction, which states that you can attract positive experiences by focusing on the positive.

You can achieve any manifestation formula with these five techniques.

A Strong Desire

Manifestation begins by recognizing your goals. What are your deepest desires? What consumes your thoughts? What aspects of your life do you want to improve or change? Self-reflect to find what goals you want to achieve. It should be something you need and not a whim. Differentiate between your wants and needs to find your true purpose. Find something significant that transforms your life or makes you feel complete, like a soulmate or a fulfilling career.

Try meditation or journaling if you struggle to find your deepest desire. These techniques clear your mind and help you visualize the life you want. Once you find your goal, focus your energy, thoughts, and emotions on it. This amplifies your manifestation and sends a loud and powerful signal to the universe. The law of attraction suggests that like attracts like. Focusing completely on your desire will attract the experiences, opportunities, and people that bring you closer to your goal.

Positivity

Fuel your desire with positive emotions and thoughts. Sometimes, people feel pessimistic when they think about their goals. For instance, a person who dreams about traveling the world may view this goal with a defeated spirit. Instead of picturing themselves traveling and having fun, they tell themselves, "I will never be able to save money and travel anywhere. I should give up and stop thinking about it." This mindset prevents you from manifesting and making an effort to achieve your goal.

You need to visualize your dream coming true and all the positive emotions you will experience when it does. For instance, if your goal is to find your soulmate, imagine how it feels to be in love and how happy you feel that you have finally found them. Positive emotions are powerful and release a high frequency that resonates with your goals and interacts with the world around you.

Belief

Conviction is key in manifestation. Believe that your desire will be manifested and release any self-doubt. Manifestation goes beyond wishful thinking. Knowing that the universe will turn it into reality once you manifest your desire. Nothing and no one can shake your trust in the process. Remember that whatever you send to the universe will come back to you. A manifestation filled with uncertainties will have low frequency and be ineffective. It is as if you're speaking to someone in a voice so low that they can't hear you.

Believing in what you say and knowing it will be manifested sends a powerful signal to the universe that cannot be ignored.

No Deadline

Manifestation formulas don't have a deadline. If your dreams don't manifest in a few months, this doesn't mean they will never become real. The universe is wise, infinite, and knowledgeable. It doesn't have the same limitations people do, nor does it work within a certain time frame. It has its own process and pace, so be patient. Maybe it wants you to learn a lesson first or experience something to prepare you before you receive your desire.

Many expect their desires to manifest right away. When they don't, they stop manifesting or doubting the universe or their abilities. This can disrupt the manifestation process. Believe that your desires will manifest without worrying about when. Everything is in motion the moment you set your intentions. The universe is preparing opportunities, events, and situations to bring you closer to your goal.

You don't have to understand how the universe works or why it makes you wait. Just trust in the process. Everything happens at the right time and not a moment sooner.

Keep Repeating Affirmations

Affirmations are the foundation of manifestation. The stronger they are, the more powerful your manifestation will be. Don't just say them once and expect your desire to be realized. Each repetition strengthens the vibrations you send to the universe and amplifies your manifestation. Repeat your affirmations every day, even if it takes months or years for your dreams to become a reality.

The Science Behind Manifesting with Thoughts

Most people consider manifestation a spiritual technique. However, others view it from a psychological or scientific approach. They believe that intention and mindset can impact a person's behavior and actions. Neuroscientist Dr. James R. Doty says that manifestation goes beyond sending positive vibrations to the universe. It is a powerful technique that can rewire your brain and train your subconscious to recognize your goals and take the necessary steps to achieve them. Say you hate your current job. Repeating positive affirmations such as, "My career fulfills me and allows me to be creative and express myself," will convince you that you will find a better job that aligns with your passion. This technique strengthens your brain pathways and motivates you to chase your goals. It also teaches your brain to prioritize your dreams so that it becomes focused on making them a reality. Dr. Doty adds that intention and visualization activate your cognitive brain networks and push you to work hard to achieve your goals.

Dr. Doty also explains that the brain creates neural connections based on experiences, emotions, and thoughts. The brain rewires itself through repeated thought patterns, focusing, and expectations.

Psychologist Dr. Carol Dweck echoes Dr. Doty's theories. You are more likely to achieve something if you believe you can do it because you will work harder and won't give up, no matter how many challenges you face.

For instance, if you believe you will get a job, you will research the company, dress nicely for the interview, and confidently answer each question. On the other hand, if you don't believe you will get it, you won't prepare for the interview and give short answers that show your lack of interest in the job.

Psychologist Barbara Fredrickson explains that positive emotions make people more creative. Psychology professor Sonja Lyubomirsky says that happiness leads to success. A positive attitude encourages people to recognize opportunities and see challenges as stepping stones.

According to a 2006 study conducted by Duke University, Fuqua School of Business, Durham, and the National Bureau of Economic Research, Cambridge, optimistic people work hard to achieve their goals. They are usually more financially stable because they save money.

The Placebo Effect

The placebo effect is a phenomenon in which a treatment, such as medication or practicing techniques like manifestation, can make one feel better or provide the desired outcome even though it has no medical or therapeutic effect. These outcomes emphasize the significance of thoughts and beliefs and their impact on one's perception and well-being.

Manifestation is similar to the placebo effect as both show that your beliefs can influence outcomes. Believing that manifestation can help you achieve your goals can affect your mindset, like the placebo effect. While the placebo effect is popular and effective, it has its limitations and can't be applied to every situation. Similarly, manifestation has its boundaries. It makes you resilient, optimistic, motivated, and confident and rewires your brain, but you won't get results without taking action.

You must understand the impact and limitations of manifestation and how it is compared to the placebo effect. While both showcase the impact of beliefs and a positive mindset, you can't depend on them alone. You need to have a plan and work hard on your dreams while believing that the universe will provide the opportunities and people needed to help you achieve them.

Neuroplasticity

Neuroplasticity is the brain's ability to rewire neural connections. Simply, it can make your brain more flexible. Your brain can change and adapt to create different reactions and responses that can benefit you. For instance, you can teach your brain to adjust plans and try again when you fail instead of giving up and feeling defeated. Repeated thought patterns and expectations can influence the brain to shape reality. Intentions, positive thinking, and repeating affirmations can create new circuits in the brain that release thoughts and emotions that no longer serve you and replace them with beneficial ones.

Focusing on the positive can alter your brain and strengthen the parts that can help you learn, act, believe in yourself, and achieve your goals. While your brain adapts to new changes, it will adjust your thought patterns and behavior, bringing positive outcomes.

The Impact of Focused Intention

Focused intention goes beyond repeating positive statements and sending them out to the universe. It is a powerful tool that can pave the way to success. It eliminates negative thoughts, self-doubt, your inner critic, and other people's opinions. It keeps you determined and optimistic, believing nothing can stand between you and your goals. Focused intention is different from regular intentions. You don't just say once what you hope to achieve. You repeat it every day to send strong signals to the universe, attracting people and situations that align with your goal. The more you repeat your intention, the more your brain will realize its significance and shift its attention to that goal to create the desired outcome.

Quantum Universe and the Multiverse Concept

If you are a comic book fan, the multiverse concept may not be new to you. Although it may seem far-fetched, many scientists and physicists claim it is possible. In quantum mechanics, particles can exist in different states simultaneously. According to the multiverse theory, when one state is observed, another quantum outcome becomes a reality in a different world. Thus, the universe branches out different alternatives or realities at each moment; these universes are separate and will never interact with one another. The result? *Different versions of your goals may already exist.*

Quantum Entanglement

Quantum entanglement is the theory that two or more particles can be entangled even if they don't exist in the same place. This led many physicists to believe in the existence of the multiverse. According to physicist Hugh Everet, the universe splits into multiple branches representing various outcomes during quantum measurement. A parallel universe is created in each branch.

Similar to particles being entangled, focusing your emotions, thoughts, and energy on your desire creates an entanglement with it.

The Observer Effect

The observer effect suggests that a situation or phenomenon can change by observing it. For instance, a person may change their behavior if they know they are being observed, such as employees working harder because their boss is watching them on camera. This theory can be applied to manifestation. Focusing on your goals can impact their outcome. You can change your reality by giving all your attention to your goals.

Alternate Realities

Alternate realities are the belief that a parallel universe exists similar to this one. You can use this theory in manifestation by believing there are different versions of reality and infinite possibilities of outcomes. Visualize yourself in any of those realities, living your life as if your desires are manifested.

The Power of Belief and Emotional Alignment

Manifestation won't work without belief. You will never achieve your goals if you don't believe in yourself and the universe. Belief is what separates manifestation from wishful thinking. Wishful thinking isn't always realistic. You simply close your eyes and daydream of different scenarios or make a wish without any emotional attachment. For instance, you can wish to become a famous singer and imagine yourself singing on stage and having fans fawning over you. It is fun to think about, but you don't believe it will happen and don't take any action to make it a reality.

Belief makes your manifestation powerful and effective. You know what you want will become a reality, and you are willing to act and work hard to achieve your goals. You are confident and trust that the universe is on your side.

Emotional alignment is also significant. Your emotions determine your vibrational frequencies. Make sure your emotions are positive and align them with your intentions to amplify your manifestation.

Practical Instructions

Energy Check

Make it a habit every day to evaluate your emotional and vibrational state. Pause what you are doing, close your eyes, and assess how you feel. If you are experiencing negative thoughts and emotions, shift your focus toward a more positive frequency. You can watch a funny video, spend time with a loved one, play with your pet, read a book, listen to music, visualize a peaceful and happy scenario, or do anything to improve your mood.

The life you are dreaming of can be a few affirmations away. Manifestation is a powerful tool that can help make your dreams a reality. While some skeptics may find it unrealistic or impractical, various psychologists have found it effective. Manifestation alters your brain through intention and positive thinking. You will start to believe in yourself and your abilities. Instead of thinking the world is against you, you will believe that the universe is working with you to bring you closer to the life you have always wanted.

Chapter 2: Shaping Your Manifestation Mindset

Having a positive mindset is crucial for successful manifestation. However, this can be challenging for some people. You may struggle with maintaining a positive attitude if you usually face setbacks in life. Limiting beliefs can make you believe that your situation will never improve. Low self-esteem and negative past experiences can make you doubt your abilities. However, you shouldn't give in to negative thinking. You should change your thought pattern and believe in yourself and the universe.

Having a positive mindset is crucial for successful manifestation.[26]

This chapter explains the role of mindset in manifestation, provides strategies for challenging limiting beliefs, and explores how to cultivate emotional alignment and build resilience.

The Role of Mindset in Manifestation

A mindset is the attitude, thoughts, and beliefs that shape your perception and worldview. It impacts every aspect of your life, including behavior, emotions, and thoughts. A positive mindset is the foundation for manifestation practices. It fuels your intention, encourages you to believe in your abilities, and motivates you to follow your dreams.

There are two types of mindsets: a growth mindset and a fixed mindset. Psychologist Dr. Carol Dweck explains that people with a fixed mindset believe their characters and abilities, such as creativity, intelligence, and strength, are static. They don't believe in growing or changing, which can prevent them from unlocking their true potential. A fixed mindset is usually the result of low self-esteem or poor upbringing.

For instance, a physically weak person with a fixed mindset wishes they were strong. Their friends tell them this can be achieved by working out and eating healthily. However, they believe they are destined to spend their life with limited physical abilities and don't do anything to strengthen their bodies.

These individuals give up when they fail or face setbacks because they believe change and growth aren't possible.

On the other hand, people with a growth mindset constantly work on growing, evolving, and improving their skills. These individuals thrive on challenges and don't let their failures define them. They trust their abilities and see mistakes as opportunities for learning and evolving. They don't allow their emotions or past mistakes to impact their positive attitude. Their growth mindset motivates them to follow their passion and overcome obstacles.

The outcome of your manifestation depends on your mindset. You can set intentions, repeat affirmations, and practice visualization for months, but you won't see any results if you have a fixed or negative mindset. Your thoughts impact your emotions, your emotions influence your behavior and actions, and your actions determine the outcome of your manifestation.

A growth mindset allows you to visualize your goals and repeat affirmations confidently. It pushes you to be more resilient, positive, and focused. You learn to become optimistic and envision yourself growing and succeeding. A growth mindset allows you to align your energy with your desire and prevents negative thoughts and emotions from deterring you.

Manifestation begins in the mind. You won't be able to practice visualization or manifest your desires if you can't picture yourself as happy, accomplished, and successful. Your beliefs and attitude can either attract or repel your goals.

Manifestation focuses on your beliefs in yourself and the universe. Your positive attitude and strong beliefs will amplify your manifestation, as you will send high frequencies to the universe, allowing you to manifest and attract everything you want. Negative beliefs and attitudes release low frequencies. You will be sending out self-doubt and negative thoughts, which will repel what you desire.

Identifying Limiting Beliefs

Limiting beliefs are negative thoughts you believe to be true. They can discourage you from pursuing your goals or trusting in your abilities. These beliefs could be about money, ideas, world issues, your job, or others' jobs. For instance, if you think money is the root of all evil or will never bring you happiness, you will not pursue high-paying jobs or ask for a raise.

Limiting beliefs can hold you back and prevent you from seizing opportunities, getting out of your comfort zone, forming healthy relationships, and changing your life. These beliefs can act as a defense mechanism to protect you from disappointments. For instance, you may stop believing in love if a loved one breaks your heart to protect yourself from further pain.

Various common limiting beliefs prevent successful manifestation. Identifying and challenging these beliefs is key to unlocking one's manifesting potential.

"I Can't Do This"

How many times have you told yourself that you can't do something? For example, you have a job interview and keep saying you are so nervous that you don't think you can do this. Or you want to get fit but don't believe you can lose weight. Do you think you will achieve any of your goals with this defeated mindset?

This belief stems from your inner critic, who makes you question your abilities. It is one of people's most common negative thoughts, discouraging them from taking chances or going after what they want.

Believe in yourself and your abilities to overcome this belief. Push through moments of self-doubt and say, "I can do this" or "I am capable of achieving my goals" instead of "I can't" each time you face a difficulty.

"I Am Not Worthy of Love"

Suppose your parents are abusive or neglectful, or you are a victim of a toxic relationship. In that case, you will believe that you aren't worthy of love. This belief will ruin your relationships. You will push people away and will struggle with trusting others. You may also suffer from low self-esteem as a result of these thoughts and end up in unhealthy relationships because you don't think you deserve better.

Practice self-compassion and forgive yourself for your past mistakes. You should also consider therapy to learn to love yourself and invite happy and healthy relationships.

"I Don't Deserve This"

Say you finished a big project, and your boss praised you for a job well done. However, deep down, you don't think you deserve this appreciation. You don't feel that you have done anything special; anyone in your place would have probably done a better job. While some may mistake you for being humble, this belief stems from feelings of unworthiness and insecurity.

Keep a journal of your accomplishments as a reminder that you deserve happiness, love, and success.

"I Am Not Ready"

Say your coworker tells you that you deserve a promotion and should talk to your boss about it. Still, you don't think you are ready for the responsibility. You have probably had this thought whenever you think of chasing a goal or getting out of your comfort zone. You keep procrastinating until you feel ready.

Feeling ready is a state of mind, not a fact. Most people who pursue their dreams never feel ready, but they do it anyway.

This belief stems from fear of failure and insecurity. It has nothing to do with being ready. You are just afraid of trying and failing.

Don't wait until you are completely ready and start living your life. Take small steps and figure things out as you go.

"This Is Difficult"

How often have you given up before finishing a task because it was difficult? Nothing in life comes easily, and hard work is necessary to achieve your goals. No one would accomplish anything if people gave up every time they faced difficulties.

When you feel that something is hard, remember all the times you succeeded and the great abilities that have gotten you where you are.

"I Can't Change" Or "Thing Don't Change"

Say your partner says you need to be more trustworthy because your lack of trust hurts your relationship. However, you tell them that this is who you are and you won't change. This mindset can impact every area of your life. Perhaps you have been in an unfulfilling job or an unhealthy relationship but can't take any steps to improve the situation because you believe you are stuck and things will never change. This belief can result in a static existence where you don't attempt to improve or grow.

Everyone has the power and ability to change and grow. Start making small changes, and you will soon notice their positive impact on your life.

"I Don't Have Time"

Say your doctor tells you that you must change your lifestyle and start eating healthily and exercising. You tell them you don't have time to work out or make healthy meals (a common belief among people with full-time jobs and families). As a result, you don't live your life to the fullest and miss out on many opportunities.

Time is the one thing people have in abundance. However, they struggle with managing it. Instead of saying, "I don't have time," say, "I will make time." Find out if you waste any time throughout the day, and make a schedule that allows you to focus on yourself and practice self-care.

"I Don't Know How to..."

How often have you used a statement that begins with, "I don't know how to."

- "I don't know how to make friends."
- "I don't know how to make a relationship work."
- "I don't know how to be happy."

Everyone goes through moments of self-doubt. They may question their skills, relationships, or future. Perhaps you believe that you don't know how to be a good parent even though you want children or how to commit to a full-time job. It is also normal to have bad days when you think you won't find happiness. However, if these thoughts are constant and impact every aspect of your life, they become limiting beliefs that hold you back in life. These thoughts aren't fixed and can be changed with therapy or self-help books.

"I Am Not Good At"

Everyone has weaknesses, and no one is good at everything. However, that doesn't mean you can't work on yourself and gain new skills. If you keep thinking that you aren't good at something, you will never learn anything new or grow. This mindset can prevent you from advancing in your career, trying new things, or improving any aspect of your life.

There is nothing in this life that you can't learn. Instead of saying. "I am not good at something," say, "I am not good at something yet." Taking classes, reading books, or researching online to gain new skills.

"I Don't Have Enough"

Many people think they don't have enough money, energy, resources, etc. Perhaps you don't think you have enough money to set aside every month or enough energy to exercise daily. This mindset prevents you from taking action and achieving your goals.

If you think you lack certain abilities or resources, find ways to improve your situation. For instance, you can ask a friend who is good with finances to give you tips on how to save money each month. If you know someone who leads a healthy lifestyle, ask them how they make time for exercising.

Other Common Limiting Beliefs

- I am not good enough.
- I am too young or too old (to achieve a specific goal).
- I will never be a good parent.
- I am not talented enough.
- I will never be one of the best (at something).
- I will never be successful.
- I don't have enough experience.
- I am not smart enough.
- No one understands me.

- I can't explain myself.
- No one listens to me.
- I never do anything right.
- If I want something done right, I have to do it myself.
- I am not confident enough.
- Everything has to be perfect.
- I can't trust anyone.
- Everything's my fault.
- No one loves me.
- I will never find love again.
- I hate people.
- Everyone is so stupid.
- I will never achieve my goals.
- I am afraid of failure.
- I don't know what I want.
- I don't fit in.
- I am too fat for this.
- I don't matter.
- No one cares about me.
- I am not good with money.
- I only work for money.
- Money is the root of all evil.
- Money doesn't buy happiness.
- I am a mess.
- It is too late to start working out or practicing self-care.
- I can't get my hopes up because I am always disappointed.
- My friends won't like the real me.
- Finding a good partner is impossible.
- Getting close to others will end in heartbreak.
- Life is hard, and there is nothing I can do about it.

- I don't deserve nice things.
- I just have bad luck.
- My looks prevent me from getting what I want.
- No one is there for me.
- I am not as good as my friends/coworkers/family.
- People will judge me.

Replacing Limiting Beliefs with Empowering Thoughts

You don't have to allow limiting beliefs to control your life. Specific strategies can help you challenge and replace these negative thoughts.

Identify Limiting Beliefs

Identifying limiting beliefs is the first step to challenging and overcoming them. However, you may struggle with recognizing these thoughts because they have been with you for so long that you have normalized them. You need to self-reflect, think of all the thoughts holding you back, and write them down.

Writing down your limiting beliefs also separates you from them. They are no longer your thoughts but words on paper that you can analyze without emotional attachment, giving you an objective view.

Find Their Origin

After recognizing your limiting beliefs, look for their origin. Where did these thoughts come from? What situations trigger them? For instance, you believe that you aren't good enough. Perhaps your parents never made you feel appreciated, pointed out your flaws, destroyed your self-esteem, or made you earn their love. Maybe you have been in an abusive relationship, and your partner manipulated and gaslighted you to feel superior.

You can't overcome limiting beliefs without first understanding their *origins*. This will help you avoid triggering situations or people who make you feel bad about yourself.

Challenge Your Limiting Beliefs

Read the limiting beliefs you wrote out loud to determine which ones are real and which ones are negative thoughts that prevent successful manifestation. Negative thoughts are easily recognized because they aren't based on facts. For instance, you believe that nobody loves you. However, if you assess this belief, you will realize it isn't true. You will find that your friends, family, neighbors, coworkers, etc., love and care about you. Evaluate each belief and find evidence to support its falsehood.

Ask yourself these questions.

- What facts support these beliefs?
- Are these beliefs grounded?
- Have you always had these beliefs? If not, what or who made you feel this way?
- Is there evidence that can contradict these thoughts?
- What would happen if you started thinking the opposite of these beliefs?
- Do these beliefs hold you back or push you forward?

Rephrasing Limiting Beliefs into a Constructive Belief

Don't accept these beliefs as facts or let them ruin your life. Challenge and rephrase these thoughts with helpful and constructive ones. Think of beliefs that boost your self-esteem and improve your life. You can use affirmation to change your thought pattern, such as "I am enough" or "I am strong and capable." Repeat these statements out loud to reassure yourself and replace negative thoughts with positive ones.

You can also reframe these thoughts by contradicting them. For instance, you can change "I don't have what it takes to get promoted" to "I am a hard worker and have the necessary skills to advance in my career." You can also change "I don't have time to exercise and practice self-care" to "I can manage my time to focus on my health."

Take Action

Start implementing your new mindset in every aspect of your life. Challenge and rephrase any limited beliefs you experience throughout the day into positive thoughts. Use statements or affirmations that allow you to create the reality you have always wanted. Once you overcome these beliefs, you can manifest your desires and believe they will become reality.

Benefits of Empowering (Positive) Beliefs

Empowering beliefs can transform your life. They can boost your self-esteem and your mood. These beliefs motivate you to pursue and achieve your goals. They push you to get out of your comfort zone and grow to become the best version of yourself. You will notice the impact of these beliefs when you find inspiration, strength, and positive energy in every area of your life.

Characteristics of Empowering Beliefs

- They motivate you and make you feel secure.
- They push you to take action and change your life.
- They help you reach your full potential.
- They don't hold you back. You will have the courage to take risks, learn new skills, and grow.

Cultivating Emotional Alignment

Aligning your emotions with your intention raises its frequency, infusing your intention with energy and amplifying your manifestation. Emotional alignment connects you with the universe and your authentic self. It provides you with the calmness and clarity required for manifestation. Positive emotions have a high frequency, strengthening your manifestation. They also act as a catalyst for bringing your dreams to reality.

Emotions connect your intentions with your desires. You can establish a vibrational alignment with your goals if you feel joy or gratitude. However, negative feelings, such as fear or doubt, can block manifestation.

How to Cultivate Emotional Alignment?

- **Positive Thinking:** Challenge negative thoughts by reframing them with positive and empowering beliefs. Remove clutter, use incense, and play soft music to create a positive environment at home and work. Surround yourself with positive people who lift you and remind you of what you are capable of and how amazing you are.

- **Emotional Regulation:** Life is filled with stressful situations, and it is easy to get lost in them. You may lose your temper, feel anxious, or get frustrated. Repeating positive affirmations, meditation, breathing exercises, journaling, and practicing gratitude can help you manage your emotions and facilitate emotional alignment.

- **Setting Clear Intentions:** Recognizing the goals you want to manifest ensures that your thoughts, emotions, and actions align with your intentions.

- **Practicing Mindfulness:** Mindful exercises such as yoga and meditation keep you focused on the present moment and foster alignment.
- **Self-awareness:** Check in with yourself multiple times a day to reflect on your feelings. If you struggle to recognize your emotions, practice meditation or journaling. When you are aware of your emotions, you can easily align them with your intentions and manifest your desires.

Building Self-Trust and Resilience

Manifestation is a journey that can be long and complex. You will be in a rush when you have a goal you want to achieve. You will want the universe to answer you right away. However, you may experience self-doubt if it takes a long time for your desires to manifest. You may think you don't have what it takes to work with the universe to achieve your goals.

Be resilient and treat every challenge as an opportunity.[87]

However, achieving your goals and manifesting your desires can take a long time - but this doesn't reflect on your skills and abilities. You should never give up on yourself or your goals. Trust that you have what it takes to make your dreams a reality. Keep working hard and trust yourself, the universe, and the manifestation process. The road to success is never easy. You may experience challenges and setbacks - but don't give up on your dreams. Be resilient and treat every challenge as an opportunity to learn and gain new skills. Maintain faith in the journey, even when the results aren't immediate.

Tips on Maintaining Faith in the Manifestation Journey

- Practice mindfulness exercises such as meditation, yoga, and breathing techniques to reduce stress and gain mental clarity. These practices will help you focus on the present moment, making you less worried about the future and remaining patient when your desires take time to manifest.

- Change your perspective. Instead of feeling frustrated that your goals haven't manifested yet, trust in the universe. Understand that it is making you wait for a reason. Keep working hard, learn from your mistakes, and have faith in its timing.

- Perhaps you are doing something blocking your manifestation, such as having negative thoughts, losing faith in the universe, or not being consistent with your manifestation practices. The universe will never abandon you, so evaluate your emotional alignment, intentions, or manifestation practices, make the necessary changes, and try again. Maybe you only depend on manifestation and aren't working to achieve your goals. Make a plan and see what you need to do to help manifest your desires, such as learning new skills, exercising, working more hours, etc.

- Remember, you should always believe that your desires will manifest. Act like your dreams have already come true, even if it takes the universe longer than you hope. Have faith in the manifestation process.

Tips to Build Self-Trust

- Be yourself without worrying about other people's judgment.
- Don't manifest unrealistic goals. They will be impossible to achieve, and you will feel discouraged and lose faith in your abilities.
- Stand by your decisions, and don't question them. Believe that you have the skills and abilities to make the right choices.
- Instead of losing faith in your abilities, strengthen your weaknesses and cultivate new skills.
- Don't listen to your inner critic. The voice behind your negative thoughts wants to destroy your self-esteem. Reframe those

thoughts by repeating affirmations or finding evidence to contradict them.
- Practice self-compassion and kindness. Forgive yourself for your mistakes, speak kindly to and about yourself, and don't tolerate disrespect from others.

Tips to Build Resilience
- Find a sense of purpose and only focus on your goals.
- Learn from your mistakes and take responsibility for your actions.
- Resilient people are optimistic. They have faith in themselves and the universe no matter how bad things get, and they maintain a hopeful mindset in the face of adversity.
- Develop problem-solving skills that allow you to fix any issue and prevent you from feeling nervous or stressed.
- Change is the only constant thing in life. Don't fight it and embrace it. Life may take you in different directions, so trust the journey and the universe.
- Resilient individuals don't allow their past mistakes to dictate their behavior. They find healthy coping mechanisms to deal with their mistakes and regrets and leave the past behind.
- They aren't passive individuals. They act to change their lives and make strategic plans for a better future.
- Resilient people don't hesitate to ask for help when they need it. They understand that it takes courage and confidence to reach out to someone when they are struggling.

Practical Instructions

Limiting Beliefs Worksheet

Use this worksheet to identify limiting beliefs, explore their origins, and reframe them as supportive, positive beliefs.

LIMITING BELIEFS	THEIR ORIGINS	POSITIVE BELIEFS

Let go of your limiting beliefs, which hold you back and prevent you from unlocking your manifestation potential. Reframe negative beliefs and replace them with positive thoughts. Align your emotions with your intentions to strengthen your manifestation. Boost your self-esteem and resilience, and believe the universe won't abandon you.

Chapter 3: Creating Your Manifestation Toolkit

Manifestation is an interesting experience that involves multiple practices that can bring your dreams to life. Now that you have learned about its impact on your thoughts and understand how to challenge negative beliefs that can block your intention, you are ready to start manifesting.

This chapter provides various tools that can enhance the manifestation process. You will explore each one and learn about their purposes. You will also find multiple exercises to apply what you learned in this chapter.

The Role of Manifestation Tools

Manifestation tools play a crucial role. They help you determine your goals, make you believe they are attainable, and provide a realistic image of how it feels like to see your desire manifested. These tools are also integrated with practical goal-setting techniques to help you focus your attention and energy on achieving your dreams.

Manifestation tools can also physically represent your intentions, making them more tangible and reinforcing your focus on desired outcomes. For instance, a vision board creates a visual representation of your goals. They are no longer thoughts or images in your head but words and pictures on a wall that you can look at daily for inspiration and motivation.

Introducing Manifestation Tools

Discover various manifestation tools to create a toolkit that you can use to manifest your dreams.

Vision Boards

A vision board, also called an action board, goal board, action board, or mood board, is a collection or collage of visuals such as drawings, quotations, photographs, or pictures from magazines that physically represent your aspirations, dreams, and goals. These images should motivate you to manifest your vision.

You should place your vision board where you can often see it.[38]

Vision boards usually focus on one aspect of your life, such as your career or romantic relationships. You can also use them for your short-term and long-term goals. For instance, you can create a vision board for a trip to Paris next summer to motivate you to save money or to start a business in the next five years.

You should place your vision board where you can often see it, such as on your fridge or bedroom wall. You can also create a digital copy and keep it on your phone.

Some people are skeptical about vision boards. They don't understand how hanging a few pictures on the wall can help them achieve their goals. Vision boards are associated with the law of attraction and visualization.

Constantly looking at the physical representation of your goals allows you to align your emotions, thoughts, beliefs, and actions to accomplish them.

According to a 2019 study by the Helen Wills Neuroscience Institute, the brain associates better with visual imagery than any other type of stimuli because they are more memorable. Your brain may struggle to remember your goals if you write them down, but it will store the images collected from vision boards.

In your daily hectic life, it is easy to get distracted and forget about your dreams. However, when you look at your vision board and visualize achieving your dreams, you reinforce your goals subconsciously. Simply, it reminds you of your desires, so you do something small each day to bring yourself closer to them.

Ideas for Vision Boards
- Health goals
- Financial goals
- Career goals
- Relationships goals
- Place you want to visit
- Awards you would like to win
- Spiritual or mental growth
- Personality traits you would like to develop, such as confidence
- Hobbies
- Skills you want to learn
- Lifestyle changes
- Changing your fashion style
- Buying a new home
- New experiences
- An adventure you would like to have

Benefits of Creating a Vision Board
- Enhancing self-reflection
- Giving you a better perspective on your goals
- Reducing stress

- Motivating you to bring your dreams to life
- Clarifying your goals
- Improving your well-being
- Increasing the chances of success

Tips Before Making a Vision Board

- **Define Your Goals:** Self-reflect and decide on the goal you want to manifest.
- **Decide on a Medium:** Choose a medium for your vision board, such as a cork board, magnetic board (to stick it on the fridge), whiteboard, wire board, canvas, wooden board, cardboard, poster board, or foam board. You can also create a vision board on Pinterest, Canva, Google Slides, or PowerPoint.

Crystals

Crystals are solid materials where the molecules are formed in a repeated pattern and come in different sizes, shapes, and colors. They can help you manifest your dreams. Each has unique characteristics, energy signature, vibration, and healing properties that amplify the power of your intentions. You can use them to focus your emotions and thoughts on your desires.

Crystals can help you manifest your dreams.[29]

Each crystal has different characteristics related to manifestation and goals, such as love, success, and abundance. Choose the one you feel drawn to and harness its properties to align your vibrations and frequency with your dreams, opening a pathway to manifest your desires.

Crystals You Can Use for Manifestation

- Citrine for success
- Rose Quartz (love and harmony)
- Amethyst (Guiding your intuition)
- Labradorite (Magic)
- Sodalite (Harmony)
- Moonstone (New beginning)
- Tiger's Eye (Courage)
- Malachite (Transformation and growth)
- Lapis Lazuli (Self-reflection)
- Black Obsidian (Protection)
- Clear Quartz (Amplifies your intentions and other crystals)
- Green Aventurine (Positivity and good luck)

Journals

Writing down your goals and dreams in a journal helps you focus on them. This technique allows you to use your creativity and power of imagination to visualize the life you have always wanted and write it down as a story. For instance, if your goal is to find your soulmate, you can write your love story as if it has already happened. You can also write your intentions, daily reflections, things you are grateful for, and affirmations and positive thoughts associated with your goals.

Guided Meditations

Guided meditation can help you visualize the outcome of your desires and strengthen your brain, giving you the mental stamina to chase your dreams.

Benefits of Guided Meditation:

- Reduces negative thoughts and emotions
- Boosts your creativity
- Makes you more mindful and focused on the present

- Makes you more self-aware
- Reduces symptoms of stress and anxiety
- Helps regulate your emotions
- Provides a sense of calmness, relaxation, and peacefulness

Affirmation Cards/Oracle Cards

Affirmations are positive statements that should be repeated regularly to shift your mindset and reframe negative thoughts. Oracle cards are a deck of creative cards that offer wisdom and messages. They allow you to tap into your intuition to gain clarity. These cards guide every aspect of your life, including family, growth, ancestral healing, career, and love. They can also help you find your path and recognize your goals.

Sound Healing

Sound healing is a type of therapy that uses the vibrations of instruments, music, and other healing sounds to awaken the energy of your body, mind, and spirit and promote relaxation and healing. Sound healing can release negative energy that blocks your manifestation, awakening your intuition to connect you with your goals.

Sound healing can release negative energy.[80]

Digital Apps

Many apps offer guided meditations, sound healing, and affirmations to enhance your manifestation practices. Download them on your phone and practice manifestation anytime and anywhere.

Practical Instructions

Discover how to practice each manifestation technique on your toolkit.

Create a Vision Board
Materials:
- Images that represent your goals, such as words/quotes, pictures from magazines or catalogs, photographs from family albums, sticky notes, bumper stickers, fabric swatches, business cards, drawings, doodles, stickers, postcards, digital images, newspaper clippings, printed words, hand-written words, souvenirs, colorful construction paper, scrapbook paper, cardstock, printed affirmations, posters, or clippings from books
- Ledge shelf or command strips for hanging pictures
- Safety goggles
- Staple gun
- Map pins or straight pins
- A piece of fabric six inches larger than your board
- A piece of Homasote board or foam adhesive squares the same size as the space where you will hang the vision board
- Adhesive tools such as poster putty, adhesive putty, hot glue gun, thumbtacks, washi tape, rubber cement, or glue sticks
- Trims or ribbons
- Ink pads or stamps
- Alphabet stencils
- Hole punch
- Paper trimmer or paper cutter
- Scissors

Instructions:
1. Organize the materials you will use on the board, such as pictures, newspaper clippings, postcards, etc.
2. If you have different goals, divide your board into categories, such as travel, relationships, and career.

3. Arrange the images artistically or randomly, but leave an adequate space between them to avoid cluttering the board. You can also add an image in the center representing an important aspect of your goal. Make sure it is aesthetically pleasing so you would feel happy and relaxed when you look at it.
4. Use large images for your main goals and smaller ones for your less important desires.
5. Place your most inspiring images at eye level or in the center. Arrange the secondary images around the main image or in the corners.
6. Choose a color palette for your board to create visual harmony. Use background color or contrasting hues to make the images stand out.
7. Add the stamps, quotes on colored paper, fabrics, etc. Layer the images in a visually appealing way. Keep your vision board exciting by playing with different layout options until you find one that feels right.
8. After you finish the layout, secure the items with glue, clips, or pins. If you plan to adjust the board in the future, avoid using glue because it's permanent.
9. Place your vision board in an accessible place where you can easily see it, such as your nightstand, across from your bed, on the back of your front door, in your home office, on your mirror, an altar, your fridge, or an empty wall in the kitchen.
10. Once you achieve your goals, remove the images and add different ones representing a new desire.
11. Place images of your goals in a box or a scrapbook to remind yourself of your capabilities and victories.

Crystal Programming for Manifestation
Instructions:
1. Choose a crystal that aligns with your intentions. Use more than one crystal if you have multiple goals.
2. Cleanse your crystal with water or selenite, or smudge it with palo santo or sage.
3. Focus on the goal you want to manifest. Hold your crystal close and visualize the goal as if it has already happened. Repeat your intention in your mind or out loud.

4. Charge your crystal by placing it under the moonlight or sunlight for several hours to strengthen its effectiveness and increase its energy.
5. Keep the crystal with you at all times. You can wear it as a necklace or put it in your wallet or pocket. Repeat your intention each time you touch the crystal.
6. Meditate with the crystal every day, repeating your intentions to amplify your manifestation and strengthen your relationship with it.
7. Align your intentions with your actions and work on achieving your goals.

Crystal Grid

A crystal grid can help you channel joy, inspiration, courage, and energy and cleanse you from any spiritual or physical issues. It arranges various crystals in a specific pattern to amplify their energy.

Instructions:
1. Define your intention.
2. Choose the grid you want to use. You will find various patterns online.
3. Write your intention on a piece of paper or use a picture that represents your goal.
4. Choose a crystal to be the focus stone of your grid. It should bring energy into the grid that aligns with your goal.
5. Choose desired stones to place them on the grid's edge to bring harmony and energy.
6. Cleanse and charge the crystals with the previous instructions.
7. Choose a location for your grid. For instance, if you want to advance in your career, leave the grid at your office. Place it near a window, as the crystals need sunlight.
8. After you put the grid in the chosen area, place the crystals on it.
9. Focus on your intention and feel your energy flowing in each crystal.
10. Activate your crystal grid by visualizing universal energy flowing through your focal crystal. Imagine you are tracing the grid's outline to connect the crystals. Follow the pattern with your mind or visualize you are tracing it with your finger.

11. After you finish outlining, repeat your intention and visualize your goal. Make sure your visualization is vivid and engages all your senses.
12. After activating the grid, leave it in its place until your desire is manifested. However, crystals absorb the energy surrounding them. Cleanse them occasionally with sage to release negative energy, or their powers will be blocked.

Manifestation Journaling

Tips for Manifestation Journaling

- Choose whether you want to write in a regular or digital journal.
- Assign time for journaling and incorporate it into your daily routine.
- Find a calm and relaxing room with no distractions to focus on your writing.
- Write, doodle, or draw your visualizations.
- You can add images to personalize your journal.

Prompts to Clarify Intentions

1. What do you value most in life?

_____
_____
_____
_____

2. Where do you see yourself in the next five years?

_____
_____
_____
_____

3. What would your life be like now if money wasn't an issue?

_____
_____
_____
_____

4. What do you want to achieve next year?

_____
_____
_____
_____

5. How will your life change if you achieve your goals? How will you feel?

_____
_____
_____
_____

6. What is your passion?

_____
_____
_____
_____

7. What excites you about your goals

_____
_____
_____
_____

8. How will you commit to achieving your goals?

_____
_____
_____
_____

9. What were your childhood dreams?

_____
_____
_____
_____

10. What makes you feel alive?

_____
_____
_____
_____

11. What habits or routines can help you achieve your goals?

_____
_____
_____
_____

12. What skills do you need to achieve your goals?

_____
_____
_____
_____

13. What changes do you need to implement to manifest your desires?

_____
_____
_____
_____

14. What challenges do you think you will face? How will you overcome them?

_____
_____
_____
_____

Express Your Gratitude

Imagine that you have achieved your goals. You are happy and grateful now that all your dreams have come true. Express your gratitude to the universe for helping you manifest your dreams.

_____
_____
_____
_____

Guided Meditation for Abundance
Instructions:
1. Find a quiet and relaxing place with no distractions.
2. Sit with purpose and close your eyes.
3. Take long and deep breaths.
4. Focus on your breathing.
5. Inhale through your nostrils while counting to four, and exhale while counting to four, too.
6. Repeat four times.
7. Feel grateful for each breath you take.

8. Feel your body and mind relaxing.
9. Keep focused on the present.
10. Express gratitude for everything you have, like your career, health, home, partner, family, friends, children, and clothes.
11. What are you grateful for? Who are you grateful for?
12. Be grateful for everything you have and for being here at this moment.
13. Align yourself with a higher vibration to connect your frequency with an abundance mindset.
14. Notice your thoughts and allow yourself to experience different positive thoughts and emotions, such as love, empowerment, appreciation, hopefulness, passion, happiness, joy, enthusiasm, optimism, creativity, and gratitude.
15. If you experience negative thoughts that lower your frequency, practice gratitude and remember all your blessings to raise your vibration.
16. Think of the goals you want to achieve to give yourself hope.
17. Feel the passion, appreciation, empowerment, and abundance.
18. After raising your vibration, ask yourself, "What do you want to manifest?"
19. Experience how it feels to achieve your goals.
20. You need to believe that you will manifest your dreams one day.
21. You need to become what you manifest. Believe that you deserve it.
22. If you desire happiness, feel happy. If you desire abundance, feel the abundance. If you desire love, feel the love.
23. Feel the emotions associated with your goals.
24. You are now in alignment with a high vibrational state. Everything you want is coming to you. Prepare yourself to receive it.
25. Don't think of how this will happen, and trust the universe. Be brave to take steps every day to achieve your goals.

Making Affirmation Cards
Materials:
- Paper
- Pen
- Affirmations
- Scissors
- Crayons, markers, and paint
- Stickers, glue, and glitter

Instructions
1. Write down ten affirmations that are associated with the goal you want to achieve, such as, "I attract love wherever I go, "I am enough," "I am healing," "My body is perfect for me," and "My life is filled with abundance."
2. If you want to create digital cards, find interesting designs for your affirmations deck. Procreate app and website have a great collection.
3. To make DIY cards, write the affirmation on paper.
4. Fold the paper or cut it into a card-sized rectangle.
5. Adorn the cards by adding stickers, glitter, or drawing on them.
6. Shuffle the cards and choose the one you feel connected to without looking.
7. Consider this affirmation a message from the universe.
8. You can choose more than one card if you want.
9. Repeat the affirmations for the rest of the day or week.

Use the same instructions to create Oracle cards, but you must make adjustments.
1. Choose a pattern for the back of the cards and draw them on the paper.
2. Brainstorm themes for your Oracle cards. Write down any ideas that come to mind, such as poetry, quotes, food, people you admire, musicians, book characters, or shapes.
3. Assign a theme to each card.
4. Decorate the cards.

5. Connect with the cards and notice how you feel and think when you hold each card. Perhaps you see an image or a person when you close your eyes. Write down your observations and use them to assign meaning to each card.
6. After you finish, turn them over and pick a card. Reflect on the card's meaning and consider it a message from the universe.

Sound Healing
Instructions:
1. Sit on a comfortable chair or lie down on the bed.
2. Put on your headphones and listen to binaural sounds.
3. Close your eyes and only focus on your breathing.
4. Visualize your desire vividly and experience the feeling of seeing it manifested.
5. Remain in this state for as long as you want.
6. After you finish, take a few deep breaths and open your eyes.

Music and Frequencies
- 963 Hz: Enlightenment
- 852 Hz: Awakens your intuition.
- 741 Hz Helps: Provides clarity.
- 639 Hz: Promotes love, tolerance, and understanding in relationships, creating harmony between you and your loved ones.
- 417 Hz: Removes negative energy and fills you with positivity.
- Binaural Beat: This is an auditory illusion. When you listen to two tones with different frequencies in each ear, your brain creates a third one, the binaural beat. It can be used in meditation to access the unconscious mind, relax, boost energy, and invite positive thoughts.
- Solfeggio Frequencies: Unique sound patterns that improve your physical and mental health and clarity and help you set clear intentions.

Digital Apps

- Headspace
- Calm
- Insight Timer
- Buddhify
- Breathwrk
- Smiling Mind
- Happier
- Portal
- Anxiety Solution
- Superhuman
- Simple Habit
- Aura
- Soaak
- FitMind
- Unplug Meditation
- Waking Up
- Apollo Neuro
- Muse
- The Breathing App
- Declutter the Mind
- Soundly
- Mindwell
- Balance
- Meditopia
- Ten Percent Happier
- Omvana
- The Mindfulness App
- Healthy Minds Program
- Breethe
- Sound Therapy
- Frequency
- Myndstream
- Endel
- Mindbreaks
- OpenEar's SWELL
- Moodsonic
- Sound wellness and biophilia
- I am
- Mantra
- ThinkUp
- Self Love
- Gratitude
- Motivation App
- Self Love
- Vision Board

Manifestation offers various techniques that you can easily incorporate into your daily life. These techniques allow you to recognize your goals and inspire you to work hard. They also have many health benefits, such as reducing stress and keeping you calm. Practice them every day to amplify your intentions, strengthen your manifestation, and guarantee a desired outcome.

Chapter 4: Visualizing the Life You Want

Visualization is one of the most significant and effective manifestation practices. It allows you to imagine your goals and how it feels to achieve them. However, visualization goes beyond daydreaming and wishful thinking. It requires vivid and detailed imagination, which can impact your subconscious, alter your mindset, and make you believe you can make your dreams a reality.

Visualization goes beyond daydreaming and wishful thinking.[21]

This chapter explores the impact of visualization on the brain and nervous system, the importance of engaging all senses when visualizing, the role of emotional energy, and the significance of visualizing regularly.

The Science and Power of Visualization

Some people are skeptical about visualization because they think it is an impractical technique that only involves imagining different scenarios and expecting them to become real. However, visualization is a complex process. It requires more brain power and activates the motor cortex located in the frontal lobe, which is responsible for controlling, planning, and moving. For instance, if you visualize yourself moving your arm, it activates the same area in your brain responsible for movement.

This process also activates parts of the brain tied to sensory experiences and emotions. When you vividly imagine your goals, you're priming your mind for success by aligning your thoughts, feelings, and actions. You'll feel more energized by new opportunities – and more inclined to pursue them – because you believe they're leading you closer to your vision. That belief builds confidence in your abilities and strengthens your resolve to overcome obstacles. Over time, this mindset will influence how you think, how you feel, and the choices you make each day.

The mirror neurons in your brain are cells that fire when you act or when you see someone performing a similar action. Similarly, visualizing yourself achieving your goals activates the mirror neurons, and you will feel as if you are going through the same experience. For instance, you visualize that you find your soulmate. You will feel the same excitement, strong emotions, and butterflies in your stomach in real life, as if you are in love.

Visualization releases dopamine, which provides the brain with various positive emotions such as motivation, pleasure, and satisfaction. When you visualize that you are accomplished and successful, dopamine activates the reward pathways in the brain. This motivates you to pursue your goals with persistence and high hopes.

This technique also soothes the nervous system, reduces anxiety and stress, and keeps you calm. Imagining relaxing situations or peaceful images, such as a beautiful forest or a beach, regulates the release of the cortisol hormone associated with stress and activates the brain's relaxation response. This state of mind increases resilience and inner peace.

Visualizing your goals can also reduce anxiety. Imagining yourself accomplishing everything you set your mind to enhance your emotional well-being. You will also start focusing on the joyful image in your brain and what you can do to make it real, distracting you from your worries and making you feel at ease.

It reprograms the subconscious and aligns it with your goals, driving you to work hard and achieve them. It also helps you identify your desires by visualizing vivid and detailed images of what it looks and feels like to be successful. This activity aligns your thoughts, feelings, behavior, and actions with your goals.

Engaging the Senses

You should engage your five senses in visualization exercises to make the experience feel real. Say you visualize walking on the beach and meeting your soulmate. You should imagine the whole experience in detail. Feel the warm sand beneath your feet, smell the air as it brushes on your hair and skin, listen to the sound of waves at a distance, and look around you to see the beautiful blue water and sky. You should also picture what your soulmate looks like, what they are wearing, their mannerisms, smell, smile, etc. Imagine how you feel when you see them. Are you happy, excited, nervous, etc.? You should also picture your interaction, what you say to each other, how they make you feel, etc. Create the whole experience like a movie.

Vivid visualization connects you emotionally with the image you created, making it feel *real,* as if it were happening to you. This emotional connection also activates parts of the brain responsible for action and perception, which drives you to work on your goals. Realistic and detailed visualization that involves engaging all your senses is more effective.

Visualization and Emotional Energy

Emotions amplify visualization by creating a positive feedback loop, drawing you closer to your goals through elevated vibrations and feelings. You also immerse yourself in the process as you engage your five senses, allowing you to experience how it feels to achieve your goals. Emotions add intensity and depth to your visualization, making it realistic.

Once you become emotionally attached to your visualization, it is no longer a mental image but a vivid and personal experience that draws you in and inspires you. The brain senses the connection between these emotions and the image in your head and motivates you to make it real. You will become more focused and determined to succeed.

Your emotional energy will keep you motivated. Passionate people are more likely to commit to their goals, take action, and overcome challenges. Incorporating emotions into visualization transforms them from casual fantasies to desires that drive you to act.

Consistency in Visualization Practice

Consistency is key with all manifestation practices, including visualization. Make visualization part of your daily or weekly routine to amplify your manifestation and strengthen the desired outcome. Envisioning your goals regularly and experiencing what it feels like to live the life of your dreams can be a great motivator. The emotions you feel when visualizing will be addictive, encouraging you to take action to achieve your goals.

Positive emotions also have a high frequency, strengthening your manifestation as you practice visualization.

Benefits of Visualization

- Boosts self-esteem
- Improves well being
- Enhances creativity and problem-solving skills
- Reduces stress
- Motivates you to focus and achieve your goals.

Tips to Practice Visualization Regularly

- **Set Intentions:** Defining your goals before practicing visualization will give you purpose and make the process rewarding.
- **Create a Routine:** Make time for visualization and prioritize it. Remember that thinking that you don't have time to practice self-care is a limiting belief. Visualization only takes 15 to 20 minutes, so you can easily incorporate it into your daily schedule. For instance, you can wake up 15 minutes earlier every day to practice or practice before bed.
- **Ask a Friend for Support:** Share your visualization plan with a family member or a friend. Ask them to hold you accountable if you don't commit to your visualization routine. You can also join a visualization group to interact with like-minded people and feel motivated to keep going.

Practical Instructions

The Mental Movie Technique

Create a "mental movie" of your desired future, where you are the main character achieving your goals. Visualize every detail of this movie and replay it regularly.

Tips

- Identify your goals, be specific, and write them down.
- Create a mental movie of your goal being manifested. Describe in detail how you achieved your goal, how your life has changed, and how you feel after this great accomplishment.
- Visualize while writing, make it vivid, and engage all your senses. Your writing should feel so real that you feel every emotion, listen to the sounds, experience the sights, and smell the air.
- Be very descriptive and write in the present tense.
- You should be relaxed while writing to tap into your subconscious mind and get creative.
- Sit in a quiet room with no distractions. Close your eyes, take a deep breath through your nostrils while counting to four, and exhale through your mouth while counting to eight. Repeat six times. This process will give you the peace of mind and clarity you need before writing.

Senses-Based Visualization

Visualize a specific goal, engaging all senses – sight, sound, touch, taste, and smell – to make the experience as vivid as possible. You can choose any goal you want.

This example is about getting your dream job.

Instructions:

1. Sit in a quiet room with no distractions or lie down.
2. Close your eyes and take a few deep breaths to clear your mind and relax your body.
3. Feel your troubles melt away with every breath.
4. Visualize yourself waking up in the morning to get ready for your first day at work.

5. You hear your alarm go off. You wake up with a smile because you are finally going to do something you are passionate about.
6. You take a shower and feel the warm water on your skin. You have breakfast and drink your coffee. Feel the taste of everything you are having.
7. You leave the house and get into your car. Then, you turn on the radio, and your favorite song starts playing.
8. You can hear the beautiful tune and sing along with every word.
9. You open the window and feel the cool air brush on your hair and skin.
10. You feel your heart pumping out of excitement. You have never been happier because your dream has finally come true.
11. You arrive at work, get in the elevator, and hear its soft music. The doors open, and you walk to your office.
12. You look around you and can't believe where you are. Notice every detail in the office. Look at your desk. What do you have on it? Did you add pictures of your loved ones? Did you put a special item?
13. Look at the view from the window. What do you see?
14. Take a deep breath and smell the air in the office.
15. Sit on your chair and feel the leather on your body.
16. Take a moment to appreciate where you are and what you have accomplished.
17. What do you feel? Do you feel happy, grateful, calm, or excited?
18. Allow yourself to feel at peace that you have now achieved your goal. Feel the relaxation, calmness, and joy wash through you.
19. If you want to smile, smile. If you want to cry tears of joy, cry. Allow yourself to feel your emotions.
20. Immerse yourself in this moment.
21. Stay in this vision for as long as you want.
22. After you finish, express your gratitude to the universe for helping you manifest your desire.
23. Take a few deep breaths and open your eyes.

Creating a Vision Script

Write in detail in your journal as if your goals have already been achieved, then read this "vision script" while visualizing daily.

Example: This vision script is about meeting one's soulmate.

"I can't imagine we have made it a whole year. I still remember the first day we met. We were at my best friend's wedding, and they were one of the guests. My best friend's cousin introduced us because they knew we would be perfect for each other. We shook hands, and I felt something when our hands touched each other for the first time. When we started talking, I knew they were someone special. I still remember what they were wearing and the smell of their perfume.

Although the music was loud, we could still hear each other. We had so much in common and laughed at each other's jokes. They brought me a piece of cake, and I remember the taste of the chocolate on my tongue. It was so strong. Before they left, we exchanged numbers. We went out on our first date two days later. I remember how excited and nervous I was. We laughed so hard until our stomach hurt. I never felt a connection like that in my life. I am grateful to the universe every day for letting our paths cross."

Mirror Visualization

Practice visualization in front of a mirror. Say affirmations aloud while maintaining eye contact, adding an empowering, self-affirming element to visualization.

- I can make a difference in the world.
- I can overcome any challenges that come my way.
- I deserve the best.
- I am grateful for my body.
- I am intelligent, strong, and capable.
- I am worthy of love.
- I am ready to receive love in abundance.
- I am grateful for everything I have.
- I am following my passion.
- I am going to be the best version of myself.
- I am at peace with the things that I can't control.
- I forgive myself for my mistakes.

Multi-Perspective Visualization

Visualize your goal in the first person, then switch to a third-person view (watching yourself achieve the goal), and finally visualize the scene from the perspective of someone else who is supportive, observing you succeed, such as your partner or parents.

Anchoring Visualization with Physical Cues
Instructions:

1. Find a quiet room with no distractions.
2. Sit in a comfortable position and hold a crystal with both hands.
3. Close your eyes and visualize your goal while holding the crystal to act as an anchor.
4. Engage all your senses. What do you see? What do you hear? Is there a distinctive scent that got your attention?
5. Immerse yourself in the experience. Notice how you feel now that you have achieved your goal. Where are you? Who are you talking to? How has your life changed?
6. Keep taking long and deep breaths.
7. How are you feeling? Are you happy, relieved, excited, etc.?
8. Do you want to smile, laugh, or cry tears of joy?
9. Focus on the positive emotions and let them flow through you.
10. Feel them in every part of your being.
11. Notice how you physically feel. How do positive emotions impact your body?
12. Do you have butterflies in your stomach? Are your cheeks flushed? Do you have the urge to smile?
13. Imagine yourself transforming the positive emotions into the crystal.
14. Stay with this feeling for a while.
15. After you finish, take three deep breaths and open your eyes.
16. Use the crystal outside the visualization session to instantly recall that same energy.

Layered Visualization

Break down the visualization into stages. First, visualize only the sensory aspects (sights, sounds, etc.). Then, add emotional responses and overlay empowering beliefs about the goal's achievability. Each session can focus on one layer, creating a rich, detailed vision over time.

First Session Instructions:
1. Find a quiet room with no distractions.
2. Sit in a comfortable position or lie down and close your eyes.
3. Imagine you are walking on the beach. Only focus on the sights and sounds.
4. Look up and watch the beautiful blue skies.
5. Turn your head and watch the blue water and the waves as they move toward the shore. The view is mesmerizing.
6. Listen to the sound of the waves as they move one after the next and the singing of the birds flying above.
7. Feel the warm sand under your feet and the air as it brushes through your hair. Notice the beach's unique smell. Immerse yourself in the experience.
8. Visualize seeing your soulmate walking towards you.
9. Notice how they look in detail. Their smile, body, hair, clothes, etc.
10. They approach you, and you start talking. Notice the sound of their voice, their perfume, and the color of their eyes under the sunlight.
11. Notice how all the sounds around you fade away, and you only hear their voice and the sound of their laughter.

Second Session Instructions:
1. Now, you will focus on your emotional responses.
2. You are standing on the beach with your soulmate.
3. You look into their eyes and feel complete.
4. You have never felt that way before.
5. You are happy and at peace. You are excited about your future together.
6. Feel every emotion you are experiencing.
7. Feel the love and joy filling your heart.
8. Your emotions have become so powerful that you can't help but smile in real life.
9. Focus on this moment and all the positive emotions you are experiencing.

Third Session Instructions:
1. As you stand in front of your soulmate, your emotions overwhelm you.
2. You see your goal finally achieved in front of your eyes and feel what it would be like when it is manifested.
3. You look around, and everything feels real, even the strong emotions in your heart.
4. You believe now more than ever that your goal is attainable and will one day become a reality.
5. Take a few long, deep breaths. Immerse yourself in this moment and the positive mindset you have adopted.
6. Slowly open your eyes. You now know that finding your soulmate is just a matter of time, and you are prepared to make the effort to make it happen.

Future Memory Visualization

Imagine a specific future scene in which you are celebrating your success as if it had already happened. Focus on details such as sounds, sights, and interactions. Recall this "memory" often, treating it as an event that has truly occurred.

Instructions:
1. Find a quiet room with no distractions.
2. Sit in a comfortable piston or lie down.
3. Close your eyes and imagine you have achieved one of your goals, and your loved ones are throwing a party to celebrate you.
4. You are so happy, and you can't believe it.
5. Your loved ones are happy for you.
6. They are applauding and cheering for you.
7. You can see the joy in your parents' eyes as they can't contain their happiness.
8. Your friends are hugging you and feeling overjoyed.
9. You feel their arms around you as they hold you close.
10. You can hear your loved one's laughter and the sound of champagne glasses clinking.
11. You can smell the chocolate cake they brought you. It's your favorite

12. You look around you and can feel everyone's love.
13. Your favorite song starts playing, and you and your friends start dancing.
14. As you dance and have fun, you have become very aware of where you are and what is happening.
15. You have achieved your goal. All these years of hard work, hope, and manifesting have paid off. It has finally happened.
16. Tears of joy are falling from your eyes.
17. This is how it feels like to succeed and achieve your dreams.
18. You are grateful to the universe for everything it has done for you.
19. Take three long and deep breaths and open your eyes.
20. Remember this moment anytime you feel like giving up on your goals or worry that you will never succeed. Believe that this moment will happen. It is just a matter of time.

Visualization is a powerful tool that strengthens your manifestation and transforms your life. It allows you to live the experience of achieving your goals. You see yourself happy, successful, and surrounded by people who support and celebrate you. Visualization will boost your confidence in yourself and the universe and make you believe you can achieve anything you set your mind to with the power of manifestation and hard work.

Chapter 5: Affirmations for Scripting a New Reality

So far, you've learned about the benefits of manifestation and its various methods, including using affirmation cards. You can find many affirmations across multiple sources, but none will be as powerful as the ones you create.

Manifestation and affirmation are highly personal practices. You need to rewrite internal beliefs. The cookie-cutter statements are unlikely to resonate with everyone's beliefs.

This chapter will teach you everything you need to know about affirmations, including how to create effective and personalized ones and the best practices to incorporate them.

The Science and Power of Affirmations

You might be wondering what makes positive affirmations so successful. It's all about the way your brain processes information. Whenever the brain receives new information about the outside world or from the body, this data travels through neural connections. Over time, similar and repeatedly received information leads to new neural pathways in the brain and across the body – creating a physical connection to the repeated information.

Repeating affirmations prompts your brain to create new neural pathways.[33]

More often than not, your brain will establish pathways for information related to negative outcomes because it's wired this way. It's an ingrained self-preservation mechanism protecting you from "danger" (i.e., everything that causes negative thoughts and feelings). Here is where positive statements come in. Repeating them prompts your brain to create new neural pathways linked to positive experiences and strengthen these. Once it does, your mind won't be focused solely on negative thoughts anymore – and the more you repeat the positive ones, the more your mind will return to them and disregard the negative ones.

According to the self-affirmation theory, positive affirmations are closely associated with the sense of self. People maintain a positive sense of self by reaffirming to themselves what they believe in in positive ways. You become wired to view and reassure yourself as competent and assertive through successes and achievements. This information gets stored in your subconscious. However, when something challenges this belief, the opposite gets stored, and you start to define yourself as inept. Ultimately, this ingrained negative self-definition results in low self-esteem, self-deprecating emotions and thoughts, and an overwhelming sense of incompetence and unworthiness.

Fortunately, there is a great way to subconsciously eliminate negative information and replace it with positive ones. Positive affirmation or self-affirmation can reinforce your core values and strengths (helping you form a positive sense of self) and eliminate everything that may hinder you in developing positive self-evaluation.

Repeating affirmations will give you a serious boost in self-esteem and mood, reduce your stress responses, make it more painless for you to deal with stressful situations, and even help you reach your goals easier. Manifestation is all about making goals and dreams become reality, so having a tool to reinforce your intention to manifest them positively is crucial for success. What could be a more powerful vehicle to empower your manifestation ability than reinforced positive beliefs about yourself, your values, and your competence?

Remember all those new neural pathways that form as a response to your brain learning new information? Each time your brain activates a pathway associated with positive information, two other processes are activated, too. One is linked to emotional regulation. Expressing, controlling, and developing your emotions is vital for living a healthy and fulfilled life. Positive thoughts lead to positive feelings and better control over your emotional landscape.

The more positivity you carry in your thoughts and emotions, the less reactive you'll be to emotional stimuli. And there's more; carrying positivity also improves your ability to control yourself in stressful situations, prompting you to avoid actions that may hinder your goals and prevent you from manifesting your dreams.

The other process is reward processing. Opening the self-regulatory mechanisms causes your brain to flood your system with biochemical rewards that make you feel good about yourself. And that further reinforces the positive sense of self you create with positive affirmations.

Individuals who practice self-affirmations often focus on the goals they want to achieve in the future. As they repeat the affirmative statements, their brain processes a high volume of information about their values and themselves. It reinforces their self-integrity, which causes them to strongly associate affirmative statements with the outcomes they want to manifest. Why? Because their brain keeps rewarding them for the positive stimuli they receive. By contrast, those who don't have positive affirmations in their arsenal will gain fewer rewards because their brain receives fewer positive stimuli and more negative stimuli.

After all, every individual's ultimate goal is to protect their self-integrity. Thoughts and feelings that reinforce values reinforce integrity, shielding against negative influences that threaten development. So, now you know why self-affirmation is so crucial in protecting self-integrity.

Through self-affirmation, you can strengthen your belief that you can adapt to various circumstances (even the most challenging ones), thus reinforcing a positive self-identity. However, self-identity is always in flux, as you can adapt to a broad range of roles, adding many nuances to your identity. This fundamental step helps you learn to define success in different ways, too. Success in reaching goals doesn't always look identical, even for the same individual – let alone for different people.

You may view reaching one goal as a success in one circumstance but aspire to do more in others, causing you to strive to achieve other goals to feel successful. Either way, you're developing a positive and empowered sense of self-identity by seeing yourself adapt and become successful in different circumstances.

A strong sense of self-identity doesn't mean you see yourself as perfect. It means you see yourself handling situations where you rely on your morals and values. Upholding your values while emerging victoriously greatly boosts your confidence and self-identity.

One of the fundamental aspects of positive affirmations is that they help you create reinforcement based on authentic achievements. On one hand, you're affirming achievements that warrant praise because you want to deserve the acknowledgment. Consequently, you'll act in a way that helps you earn it. On the other hand, by reinforcing positive achievements you've reached in the past, you're motivating yourself to strive for them in the future, too.

Whether you use positive affirmation to manifest your goals, aspirations, and interests or reinforce your core values or achievements, it will only work if you keep repeating the phrases over and over again. Why? It's simple. When you repeat information several times, it will ring more truthfully than anything you hear once. So, if you reaffirm positive statements time and time again, your mind will have no choice but to believe they're true.

Do you want to achieve the goals you set for yourself? Practice positive affirmations that reassure you that you'll be able to do it – or better yet, that you've already done it. This approach will give you a more positive outlook on the future, encourage you to take actionable steps to reach your goals and keep that positive reward system in constant motion.

Crafting Effective Affirmations

Want to make your affirmations more effective and powerful? Follow some of the tips below for writing impactful statements.

Start With "I"

"My" also works when referring to a positive quality you want to affirm, but affirmations starting with "I" are crucial for changing your self-perception. They make you the center of the affirmation and bring your attention to yourself, your needs, and your desires.

Always Use the Present Tense

If you think of something as if it has already happened, it will feel right. You'll feel that it will happen because it should happen. So, whenever creating affirmations for yourself, use the present tense to empower them.

For example, instead of saying, "I will work on..." say, "I am choosing to work on..."

When you say the second sentence out loud, you'll feel like it's your reality in the present time, even if it's yet to happen in the future. Yet, it's more likely to happen because you believe it will.

Be Clear and Focused

To make your statements clear and focused, consider what you want to work on. What goals do you want to concentrate on? What area of your life are they related to? What specific aspect can affirmations help you with?

For example, if you're creating affirmations for manifesting your dream job, you can say: "I'm getting closer to obtaining my dream job." It's simple, focused, and effective. Write affirmations for all your goals like this, and you can manifest them with practice.

Keep the Statements Concise

Manifestation through affirmation takes time and practice. You'll need easy-to-remember statements you can whip out and revisit at any time to empower your intention. They should be related to your goals and direct enough that you don't get them mixed up.

Enrich Them with Your Power

Do you know what's the best way to empower your affirmations? By tailoring them to yourself and your unique strengths. Do you find switching from negative thoughts to positive ones challenging but somewhat easier if you can find an alternative? If so, your affirmations should include statements that counter negativity and reinforce positive thinking.

Centering affirmations around your goals is useful, but it isn't enough. Simply focusing on a goal could make you feel that nothing else matters. If you don't reach a goal, it will only make you feel worse afterward, making you reject affirmative statements in the future because you'll think: "What's the point? It didn't work last time either."

Think about what could make it work. Perhaps you'll benefit from tying it to more empathetic and reassuring emotions. For example, instead of saying, "I'm going to work on..." say, "I'm doing my best to work toward..."

Types of Affirmations for Manifestation

You can use various types of affirmations for manifestations, from self-belief affirmations through abundance affirmations to gratitude statements and even specific goal-related affirmations. Here is what they mean and a few examples to inspire you to create your own.

Self Belief Affirmations

Believing in yourself is crucial for manifesting your desires and building the life you want. Self-belief affirmations will make you grateful for everything that has made you who you are and acknowledge that you are worthy of everything you desire. They will also encourage you to recognize your unique qualities, strengths, and weaknesses and prioritize your needs.

Here are a few examples of self-belief affirmations:

"I believe in myself."

"I'm open to exploring and accepting my needs."

"I know my strengths."

"I'm proud of who I am."

"I'm thankful for my strengths, qualities, and skills."

"I choose to be the person who can do anything they dream of."

Abundance Affirmations

These affirmations boost confidence and help you stay even more focused on the goals and positive changes you want to achieve. They also help maintain a positive mindset, making working toward the desired outcome easier. By manifesting what you want in abundance, you can also maximize your power and obtain everything you need to become the version of yourself you want to be.

A few abundance affirmations to inspire you are:

"I can obtain everything I want."

"I attract abundance."

"I can obtain what I need for success in life."

"My abilities are empowering me to create a life abundant in love, happiness, and success."

Gratitude Statements

Have you noticed all the positivity around you? Doing so will promote a more balanced mindset and steer you from manifestation-hindering negativity.

You have many achievements, blessings, strengths, and actions for which you can be thankful. So why not acknowledge them with statements like this:

"I'm grateful for my skills."

"I'm grateful for being able to live the life I do."

"I'm grateful for all the encouraging people I have in my life."

"I'm grateful for what I have achieved so far."

"I'm grateful for reaching all my goals, even the smallest ones."

Specific Goal-Related Affirmations

These affirmations must be tailored to your specific goals. For example, if you want to enhance your creativity, you need statements that make you confident in your creative skills. They need to eradicate doubts that chain your creative energy and prevent you from expressing yourself in a way that resonates with you.

For example:

"I'm unique, and my creativity is unique, too."

"I can express my creativity in many ways."

I don't let my imagination become limited by other people's ideas, beliefs, and suggestions."

"I'm inspired by everything and everyone around me."

Likewise, if you want to create affirmations for clarity, you'll need statements that enhance your focus and self-awareness and bring you insights into your core desires and needs.

For example, you can obtain clarity by saying:

"I see my dreams becoming reality."

"My mind is calm and focused."

"My thoughts are organized."

"I'm focused on making the changes I want."

"My mind is free of limiting thoughts and beliefs."

These are just some examples of goal-specific affirmations. Feel free to craft statements that align with your goals.

Personalized Affirmation Creation

Affirmations work best if they're tailored to your personal desires and needs. To ensure they are best suited for you, you'll need to do a little self-exploration and experiment with different affirmations.

Wondering how to find affirmations that resonate with your goals and needs? Here are a few tips to help you out:

- **Reflect on your core desires.** What do you want to achieve? Is there something you want to improve or obtain? What values do you want to uphold? What is preventing you from achieving your goals? Answering these questions will lead you to the intention on which your affirmations should be based.

- **Think about your negative beliefs.** Are there some thoughts that may be holding you back from fighting for your dreams and goals? Do you tell yourself you'll never reach a specific goal? Or that you don't have what it takes to attain it? By identifying these beliefs, you can craft affirmative statements to counter and replace the negativity with positive thoughts.

- **Raise your awareness of your feelings.** Reflect on challenging situations and notice how they make you feel. What are your thoughts on these feelings? For example, when facing a tough situation you can't conquer right away, do you get frustrated and think: "I'll never be able to do this?" Understanding how your feelings affect your mindset will provide insight into what positive affirmations will work the best for you. For example, suppose a slightly negative situation and feelings lead you down the path of catastrophizing. In that case, affirmative statements that challenge the "worst-case scenario" you're envisioning will be helpful.

- **Switch to the positives.** List some positive attributes once you've identified negative thoughts and emotions that may hinder you in achieving your goals. Doing this will reinforce the thought that not everything is so negative and that you have the strength to face the challenges. Alternatively, you can enlist desired outcomes associated with your goals or the positive changes you want to bring into your life. How can your positive qualities help you achieve this?

- **Start experimenting.** Write three affirmations that align with your goals based on all the negatives and positives you've identified. Use positive, reassuring language and the present tense. You can, for example, start them like this:

  "I am..."

  "I have..."

  "I choose..."

- **Make sure your statements evoke strong positive emotions and leave no room for negativity.** Write them down or say them out loud daily. Notice how they make you feel and think.

- **Tweak the affirmations.** When formulating and repeating the affirmative statements, pay attention to whether they feel authentic. What's your gut telling you about the affirmations? Do they feel right? Your intuition will guide you toward phrases that evoke inspiration and a sense of empowerment. If they don't feel right, you may need to change the wording to ensure they are suited for your unique journey, and that's all right.

Mirror Affirmations

Saying affirmations in front of a mirror can boost confidence in manifesting your desires. All you need is a mirror and your affirmations, and you can easily incorporate the exercise into your daily routine.

Saying affirmations in front of a mirror can boost confidence.[88]

Instructions:

1. Get into a comfortable seated or standing position in front of a mirror.
2. Take a deep breath and release it slowly.
3. Look into the mirror and make eye contact with yourself. Talking to yourself aloud like this will reinforce your intention and belief.
4. Start with simple affirmations like this:

    "I'm confident and capable."

    "I'm enough."

    "I feel good about myself."

    "I am worthy of my desires."

    "I'm optimistic."

    "I'm in control of my life."

5. Once you state your affirmations, sit or stand in silence for a couple of minutes. Let those statements sink into your mind and body.
6. Take a deep breath, then release it.
7. Once you can confidently repeat the simple statements, you can start gradually incorporating more specific affirmations related to your goals.

Affirmation Scripting

Sometimes, making yourself believe that what you're affirming has already happened is the hardest part, especially at the beginning of your manifestation journey. If you're struggling with this, try affirmation scripting. It requires you to write a paragraph as if your desired outcomes are already a reality, which makes you trust that it will happen. You can describe how you feel and what you've achieved and use positive language in the present tense to make you see what is going to happen.

Even if the reality turns out to be slightly different from what you've written, the process will give you a sense of control over your life. For example, suppose you're manifesting reaching a goal in a certain way, but you reach it in another way. In that case, it will still show you that you had the power to overcome whatever obstacle prevented you from reaching that goal beforehand.

Instructions:

1. Take a pen and paper (or, even better, a journal where you can record your scripts and revisit them to enhance your manifestation/visualization practice).
2. Start describing how your life will look like when you've reached your goal. Use as many details as possible. Where are you? What does this place look like? What do you think being in this place means? Who is with you? How do you feel? What beliefs or values are you sticking to in this new life?
3. You can also use specific language related to your goal. For example, if you're manifesting a financial goal (even if it is to have stable finances), say something like:

    "I'm financially stable."

    "I've reached the financial goals I set for myself."

4. Describe exactly what you want. Once you've written down your desired future, read it over. You can do this right away or set it aside until the next day and then revise it. When revisiting, check that what you've written aligns with your dreams and desires and not someone else's. Do not write anything that someone else would want you to achieve or something that would benefit someone else, even the people closest to you.
5. Later, you can make another script describing how your mindset (and reality) started to shift as you advanced on the manifestation journey. Write how your feelings and thoughts change as you start noticing the power you have in achieving your goals.
6. Write how reclaiming your power, step by step, made it easier to manifest what you've envisioned for yourself.

While mentioning specific dates for reaching your goal (or parts of your goal) is not recommended in the beginning, once you start shifting to an "I will make it happen" mindset, you can add deadlines for your goals because you'll be confident in attaining them.

Another tip is to avoid negative language. Don't write how difficult it will be to obtain your goals because it will only make you think you'll never overcome the obstacles you'll face. Remember, the thoughts and feelings you cultivate during manifestation are what you'll take with you on this journey. If you only take the positive ones, you won't leave room for negativity in your mind and spirit.

Writing about a dream reality in the present tense may seem like wishful thinking, but you'll be astonished at how much you can realistically predict. From the moment you start writing, you're changing your mindset into believing you can make it happen.

As liberating as it may feel to put your dreams into writing, it will be even more fulfilling to see yourself reaching all the goals you've described yourself achieving once you revisit your entries. You can repeat the exercise every couple of months to align your script with new goals and intentions.

Affirmations with Breathing

Effective affirmations include using both the body and mind. By pairing your affirmative statements with deep breathing exercises, you're engaging your entire being in adopting a useful conviction. Choose affirmations that resonate with you and incorporate them into the exercise below.

Instructions:

1. Stand or sit comfortably.
2. Take a deep breath through your nose. As you do, say an affirmation silently in your mind.
3. Hold your breath for 3-4 seconds, letting the statement get infused into your mind just as the air enters the parts of your body. For example, you can say something like:

    "I am attracting success."

4. Then, opening your mouth slightly (as if preparing to blow through a straw), slowly release the air from your lungs. As you do, say something like:

    "I release any doubt."

5. As you inhale again through your nose, repeat the first affirmation. Hold, then repeat the second affirmation as you exhale through your mouth. Continue until you feel that you're making the statements with a sense of conviction.
6. Do this exercise at least once a day.

Chapter 6: The 369 Method and Other Secret Manifestation Formulas

This chapter outlines the concept of manifestation formulas, including the 369 Method, a popular technique revered by Nikola Tesla, and several other unique formulas, such as the 5x5x5 formula or the 2x4 method.

Learning these techniques will enhance your manifestation practice and bring any desire to reality. Throughout the chapter, you'll also receive tips for creating personal manifestation formulas, bringing you one step closer to making manifestation come from the deepest corner of yourself and ensuring a successful result.

Understanding Manifestation Formulas

Before you start learning about specific manifestation formulas, you may be wondering what these formulas are. What makes them so effective and fundamental in manifestations?

Manifestation formulas are techniques relying on the energy of numbers. As the numbers are repeated, the person repeating them aligns their energy with the energy of the numbers. In most cases, success lies not in repeating a certain number or numbers but in using them to enhance the intention to manifest something. In other words, the numbers become key elements in writing, visualizing, and emotionally engaging with goals a person wants to manifest.

The Role of Numbers

Numbers have been linked to spiritual and even religious practices since ancient times. They are wonderful tools for harnessing spiritual wisdom, as they all have unique vibrational frequencies. They can also influence the energy and vibration of everyone and everything they're applied to. From the energies of the universe to the energy of your self-improvement and fulfillment journey, everything operates on vibrational frequencies that can be affected by other frequencies, including numerical ones. Moreover, repeating numbers amplifies their power and reinforces the intention towards which you are channeling them.

Each number is linked to a different energy.[84]

Each number is linked to a different energy, meaning they can be used in personal transformation through goal setting. By understanding which number is linked to which energy, you can align yourself with the ones that best suit your purpose. In other words, it can help you manifest whichever goal you want based on the number linked to the aspect the goal refers to.

Some numbers have a wider range to cover than others, but most have a theme their energy encompasses. Below are the core energies associated with each number and how they can help you manifest your goals and dreams:

1 - Unity: Linked to the origin of everything, number one symbolizes unity and the potential to create anything you want. If you aim to enhance your creativity and craft something unique or express yourself through it, you can use this number to manifest it. It raises self-awareness and makes you feel connected to the energies around you.

2 - Partnership: Embodying balance and harmony, number two is the perfect example of how something with two different sides can work together. It helps opposites work through their differences, so it's great for manifesting goals in a relationship (for example, strengthening trust, communication, etc.) Simultaneously, it can help you find balance within yourself, which can come in handy when your energies are out of balance.

3 - Manifestation: More specifically, the number three is linked to the manifestation of your deepest desires. It can be used in practice when you want to obtain a goal related to your inner self and show what you truly want and need to the outside, physical world.

4 - Stability: Should you need a number to manifest goals related to the material world (for example, finances), number four should be your go-to digit. It helps you build a powerful foundation to set up the pillars of your financial and personal stability. Besides personal development, this number can help you manifest goals for loved ones and community members.

5 - Transformation: Associated with change and progress, number five reminds you of the dynamic nature of life. It shows you that nature evolves – and so can you by facing and persisting through challenges. If your goal is to enhance your adaptability when facing adversities, feel free to use the number five to manifest it.

6 - Love: The number six embodies love and compassion. It is another digit that can bring harmony into your life. Whether you need harmony in the workplace, in relationships, or in creating an environment for spiritual growth, the number six can help you manifest it.

7 - Insight: If you want to raise your awareness and receptiveness to spiritual wisdom, seven might be the perfect number to call on. It inspires self-reflection and can assist in introspective exercises and explorations. It may also help you receive spiritual guidance and elevate your consciousness to a higher level.

8 - Abundance: Associated with spiritual and material abundance and infinite energy, number eight can be useful if you want to manifest goals for long-term prosperity. It may also help if your goals are to establish yourself as an authority and the source of empowerment.

9 - Completion: Embodying fulfillment and completion, number nine signifies the end of the road. If your goal is to grab that spiritual wisdom you see at the end of your journey and never let it go, use number nine to manifest it. Likewise, you can use it to consolidate efforts and practices to empower your road to fulfillment and goal completion.

10 - Renewal: After completion comes rebirth in nature, which the number ten signifies. If you're at a crossroads and want to set goals to find the way to move forward, call on number ten to manifest it. It will show you the new path you need to follow to achieve these and any other goals you may set in the future.

Manifestation Methods and Formulas

There are countless ways to manifest your desires. Below are some of the most popular manifestation techniques and a brief explanation of how they work and their unique benefits.

The 369 Method

Rooted in the principles of the law of attraction and inspired by the work of Nikola Tesla, the 369 methods surely stand out among the manifestation formulas. As in many other manifestation techniques, repeating is key in the 369 method. Writing clear affirmations three times in the morning, six times in the afternoon, and nine times in the evening over 21 days, you gain a structured way to enhance your focus on intention.

So, how does the 369 method work? Nikola Tesla claimed that the numbers three, six, and nine hold a massive significance in how the universe and its energies work. According to this theory, number three signifies the connection to higher energies, creativity, manifestation, and self-expression. It can also be viewed as a trinity of forces linking the body, mind, and spirit. Number six embodies harmony and inner strength. It's the one showing you just how powerful you are and helps you align yourself with the energy you want to manifest. It's one of the most powerful numbers in manifestation and a central tenet of the 369 method. Number nine symbolizes transformation, completing the cycle in which you can release the past and embrace the future. This new beginning number nine shows you is another crucial part of this method.

How do you use the 369 method? You do that by following a consistent routine and the steps below.

Instructions:
1. **Get a pen and a piece of paper.** Tip: Use colored markers or pens, as these will make channeling different emotions and associated energies much easier. It's like color-coding the tools for your manifestation. It's best to do that in a journal, where you can track and revisit your entries to see your progress and remain organized (so you won't skip a day or repeat).
2. **Identify your manifestation.** What goals do you want to achieve? Are you looking for a new job, relationship, spiritual growth, healing, or something else? Take a moment to think about it.
3. **Formulate your first affirmation.** It's best to focus on one affirmation reflecting one goal at a time, especially if you're a beginner. Otherwise, you can mix them up and lose focus on each one. Be specific and use the present tense when creating the affirmation. As always, you want to convey that you've already achieved what you're manifesting. Likewise, ensure that your phrase accurately describes what you want to accomplish. It doesn't have to be a long sentence (after all, you'll be repeating it through the following 21 days). Still, it should be descriptive enough to identify it with a specific goal. Avoid words like can't, won't, don't, etc. Negativity attracts negativity, and what you want is to channel positivity.
4. **Have you formulated your affirmation?** Repeat it aloud or in your mind. Does it sound believable? Is it something you can reasonably accomplish? Does it make you look forward to the future? If so, you've found the affirmation that resonates with you.
5. **Now, repeat the affirmation.** Start in the morning, as soon as you wake up. Take a deep breath and write down your affirmation three times. After each time, take 17 seconds to contemplate what thoughts and emotions the affirmation evokes in you. Your energy is being realigned, so new feelings and thoughts are bound to pop up.
6. **Sit for a few more minutes**, letting the energy of your intention reverberate through you. You've now aligned your mindset to work toward the desired goal throughout the day.
7. **Around midday, sit down again** and write your affirmation six times to reinforce the goal-oriented mindset. It will help you channel more energy into your intention, empowering it to work for you throughout the rest of the day.

8. **Write your affirmation again in the evening**, nine times on this occasion. Do this just before going to bed to solidify your subconscious intent. It will continue working on manifesting your goal while you sleep.
9. **Repeat the affirmation** three times every morning, six times every midday, and nine times every evening for an overall of 21 days.

Visualize what you want to manifest. While this is optional (and you don't have to do it during each repetition), try envisioning yourself living the reality you're trying to manifest. As you write the affirmation and let its energy infuse your intuition, imagine that what you're writing is true. Let yourself feel the emotions you associate with the desired goal. Would reaching it make you feel happy? Fulfilled? More relaxed? Whatever it is, feel it. Allow yourself to immerse in this awesome present-turned-future experience fully.

As you write, visualize, and repeat your affirmation during the 21 days, you may feel inspired to take action and engage in practices that can enhance the exercise. The power of repetition is enormous, but it can still be magnified by taking steps that align with the goal you want to manifest. For example, after writing down your affirmation in the morning or midday, you may feel inspired to decide during the day that'll bring you one step closer to your goal. Whatever choice you're encouraged to make, if it comes from your intuition, take it.

In the 369 method, nothing is coincidental. Even the number of days you repeat the affirmation has a numerological significance. Some numbers have the power to enhance the energy of others, and this is the case with number 21 as well. While some may go for longer periods (for example, 33 days), 21 days are enough for a new pattern to become completely ingrained in the brain – and this is exactly because this number empowers positive mindsets, helping to rewire the brain. During those 21 days, countless new neural pathways can form, and you'll be able to focus on your intention to manifest your goals more and more. While the method described above instructs for a 21-day practice, you can tweak it and change it to shorter or longer slots depending on your needs and goals.

If you happen to skip a day, don't worry. Unexpected circumstances can occur and cause you to change your schedule. The method isn't about obtaining the perfect score by writing your affirmation on 21 consecutive days. Does it help focus and make you feel fulfilled if you do the 3, 6, and 9 repetitions 21 days in a row? Absolutely. Will you automatically lose focus if you skip a day? Unlikely. It can happen if you skip the second or third day after completing only one, but rarely if you skip a day by the end of the 21 days.

So, what do you do if you skip a day? Acknowledge it, but don't see it as a setback. You had a bump on the road, and now it's time to get back on track. Continue where you left off (this is where writing them in a journal will come in handy), and repeat the affirmation the day after the one you skipped. Focus on staying on track during the rest of the journey.

If you frequently miss days, your focus may be hindered. Consider what this could be. What made you lose focus on your goal? How can you eliminate it? Redirect your focus to what you want to achieve and why; you'll find yourself motivated – and this will help you stay on track.

No matter whether you miss days or can complete the exercise in 21 consecutive days, maintain a positive attitude and don't let anything undermine your effort. Believe in yourself, your energy, and your ability to manifest your intent and goals.

Why must you maintain the feeling or thought evoked by the energy you are trying to manifest for 17 seconds? It's simple. It's how long it takes your intention to fully infuse your manifestation process. Your brain needs 17 seconds to link the thought it's focused on to a certain type of energy. This initial state precipitates the law of attraction at work in the 369 manifestation method. After 17 seconds, you will be aligned with positive energy, and you can start attracting similar, positive energy to yourself.

Besides repeating your affirmation in the 3,6,9 pattern, you should also strive to understand how it will help you reach your goal. You can work this out when formulating your affirmation and revisit it later when you're sitting with it after writing. What thoughts and feelings does it evoke? Do you find analyzing them helpful (use those 17 seconds to ponder on them to your advantage)?

When visualizing the goal you want to manifest, focus on the positives. Unfortunately, the brain is often better at conjuring up images that evoke negative feelings and thoughts. However, you should still do your best to disregard them and bring up only positivity. Once again, you'll attract what's in you and around you. Positive visualization attracts positivity.

Manifestation takes practice and time, so repeat the 21-day cycle when needed. You may not see the result immediately, and this is okay. Just because it doesn't happen right after 21 days doesn't mean it won't happen sometime after, even unexpectedly.

As you write and sit with your affirmations, you may receive insights or have unique ideas to implement on the rest of your manifestation journey. Write these down, too. Not only will this help you remain motivated, but it will also help you track your progress.

While the 369 method is excellent goal-development practice (it encourages focusing on one goal at a time), you can combine it with similar methods to keep track of your goals. For example, you can use it alongside guided imagery, meditation, or vision boards to manifest your goals.

The 5x5x5 Method

The 5x5x5 method relies on repeating an intention for five consecutive days to manifest changes in your life. As short as it seems, this manifestation method can lead to quite a bit of a transformation due to the frequency of the repetition (three times a day). Each time, you must write and channel the affirmations five times. (Alternatively, you can visualize your goals instead of writing the affirmations, creating a mental scene where what you affirm has become a reality.) As you do this during the five days, your subconscious becomes reprogrammed to align your energy with your goals and desires. Repetition is key to manifesting change and aligning yourself with the vibration of what you want to see yourself accomplishing.

Besides the frequency, the numbers used in this method play a crucial role in its success. As it's highly associated with transformation, number five can channel and amplify the energy of change, especially if its energy is channeled several times in a short period.

Repeating the affirmation this frequently across five days prompts your mind to focus on your intent the entire time. You become fully immersed in the energy you want to manifest, making it easier to start viewing the present-tense affirmations as if you're already experiencing the future in which your dreams have become a reality. You remain focused, and your mind starts forming new neural pathways to kickstart forming your new affirmation habit.

Instructions:
1. Dedicate a space for writing and/or reciting your affirmations. It should be quiet at any time of the day (perhaps, for the same reason, the bedroom might work best, but feel free to choose any cozy place you want). You need to be able to think and write without distractions.

2. Start in the morning as soon as possible after waking up, before your mind becomes occupied with daily worries. Light a candle or incense if it helps you focus and channel the energy you want to manifest.
3. Sit in front of your journal and think about a manifestation statement that would work best in the situation. Be specific and use positive language. For example, if you want a new work position, say, "I'm grateful for this rewarding new position."
4. When writing your statement, don't just go through the motions. Think about what makes you feel excited. Are there any words that evoke positive emotions when you hear or read them? If so, include them in your statement. The more heartfelt your affirmations are, the smaller they'll make the divide between your present and desired future.
5. Write a statement five times in a row, stopping for a few moments after each repetition and letting the words resonate with you.
6. Go about your day until midday. Now comes the challenging part – carving out time to write your affirmations another five times during midday. It's best if you already schedule your day around the practice, so you won't have any conflicting or distracting activity planned for either time during the five days.
7. After your midday repetition, continue your day until bedtime.
8. Then, write your affirmations again, five times in a row, taking a short time to align yourself after each repetition as you did during the morning and midday.
9. Repeat writing your affirmations in the next four days as well without skipping. If you skip a repetition, it's best to start over because the momentum you've been building to focus your energy on manifestation has been lost. While you can skip a day without losing focus with longer-lasting formulas, here you can't. Each day and repetition brings you closer to your goal, and each missed one takes you further away.
10. After the fifth day of using the formula, you should feel the emotions and energy associated with what you want to achieve as if you're already experiencing success. The practice creates a deep connection with the feeling of having what you want to manifest, empowering your manifestation ability.

The 5x5x5 manifestation formula builds focus and trust in your intuition. It also bridges practicality with spiritual energy. By connecting with higher vibrational frequencies, you'll quickly rewire your brain. You'll also actively channel your mind and energy to work for you in making your dreams come to life.

However, if you're a beginner, one five-day affirmation exercise likely won't do the trick. You must dedicate time, attention, and focus to manifest your goals. Yet, if you trust the process and continue practicing diligently, you can align your energy with the frequency you want to manifest. From then on, your dreams, desires, and wishes are just a few steps away.

The 2x4 Technique

The last technique in this chapter is perhaps the easiest. It's fairly simple: Write down the affirmation twice a day, four days in a row.

Instructions:
1. Place the journal at your bedside before going to bed.
2. In the morning, grab the journal and write down the affirmation you choose to manifest. Do this as quickly as possible after waking up. Don't leave yourself room to overthink. Just write it down once, take a deep breath, then write it down again.
3. Go about your day as usual.
4. Before going to bed, open your journal again and write down your affirmation two more times.
5. Leave your journal at your bedside again and repeat step 2 the next morning.
6. Repeat the ritual of writing down your affirmation twice in the morning and twice in the evening for four consecutive days.
7. After one four-day cycle, waiting a few days to see whether your manifestation has started working is a good job. If not, repeat the entire 2x4 process.

Creating a Personal Manifestation Formula

Sometimes, you may benefit more from combining elements from several manifestation techniques. Doing so can create a personal manifestation formula perfectly aligned with your values, needs, and goals. For example, the 369 method works best if you focus on one goal at a time but may have set other goals during the same period. Then, you can combine the 369 methods with another one that can help you reach your other goal(s), and you can successfully manifest all of them simultaneously.

Moreover, as manifestation is a personal journey, there is no one-size-fits-all solution. Some may benefit from one method, others from another, and yet you may find that neither works for you on its own.

So, how do you create a personalized manifestation formula? Start by determining what you want to manifest. Think of something that seems like a far-away, intangible dream you want to convert to reality. Let go of self-limiting beliefs and focus on what you want to see yourself achieving. You can even set up checkpoints to verify you're on your way to manifesting your goals. When you reach these points and goals, how do you plan to express your gratitude for your achievement? Consider this before crafting your formula. It can boost your motivation to get as creative as possible and find what resonates most with you.

Once you determine what you want, imagine your vibrational energy when you achieve it. Use your intuition to determine the frequency you desire to manifest. Channel this frequency by tapping into your energy and raising your vibrations to the desired level. Look into numbers and formulas designed to elevate vibrational frequency and use them during your practice.

Continue accessing your feelings and vibrations as you work toward manifesting your goals. After each step you take toward meeting your target, verify whether your energy matches the vibrations of what you want to experience.

Lastly, let go of biases and judgment. You may feel that certain formulas may not work for you because they aren't aligned with what you believe you want. Or, you may have tried them in the past and found that they didn't work. Either way, it's time to let go of past experiences and beliefs. You won't know whether something works in the present until you try it, and this is where the beauty of creating your personalized formula lies. If you think a formula doesn't work because a specific part doesn't align with your belief, why not try substituting that component with one from another formula? You may find that with a new combination, the formula becomes perfectly aligned with what you want, and you can finally start using it to elevate your vibrations to the frequency you want to manifest. You can mix and match until you find what works.

Chapter 7: Quantum Jumping and Reality Shifting

Taking you a step closer to finding and connecting with the version of yourself you want to be, this chapter introduces you to the concept of quantum jumping. Outlining the idea that you can shift into other realities, the chapter explores how you can jump into the future and other versions of yourself and your life where you have reached your goals and dreams. Besides learning how quantum jumping works and what role consciousness plays in it, you'll also receive helpful tips and techniques for attempting quantum jumps.

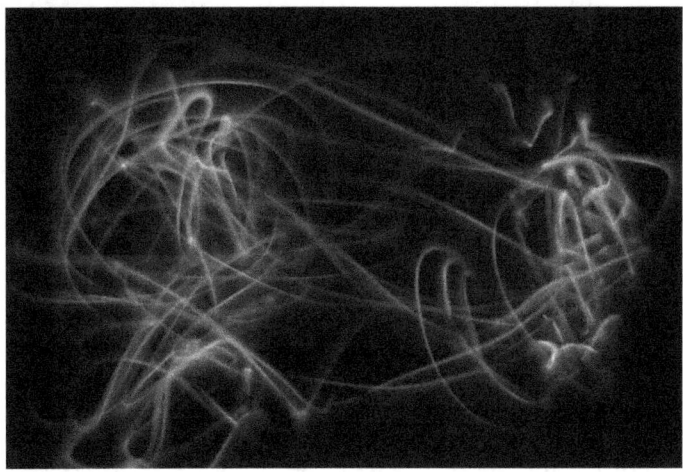

Quantum jumping is a technique that allows a person to mentally shift to another version of themselves.[85]

What Is Quantum Jumping?

Quantum jumping is a technique that allows a person to mentally shift to another version of themselves. It relies on the idea that every person has several versions of themself and can align with any version, one at a time. Just like in quantum physics, the atom can switch between two different states (for example, atoms in gases can shift between liquid and gas states), it is believed that individuals can also change from one state to another. The difference is that people have more than two versions to shift between. However, like the atom, a person can never be in two states simultaneously. If you want to connect with the different states/versions of yourself, you must practice changing from one to another. By doing this, you can harness the wisdom, strength, goal-setting skills, and anything else you need for personal and spiritual development to live a fulfilled life in your current version of yourself.

Understanding Reality Shifting

Quantum jumping involves the practice of shifting consciousness to alternate realities. These realities represent alternate timelines and spaces. How do you change your consciousness from one reality to another? You engage your focus through visualization, meditation, scripting, and other awareness-enhancing practices. The alternate realities represent opportunities for exploring personal growth, harnessing spiritual wisdom, and motivation for working toward goals you see yourself achieving in an alternate reality. It's a subjective experience that allows individuals to find guidance for manifesting desired outcomes.

To attempt reality shifting, you need to be able to immerse yourself in a visual or otherwise consciousness-altering sensory experience. You can obtain this by practicing visualization and intense focus, enhancing your imagination, and being open to experiencing and embracing new emotions. By honing these skills, you can become more susceptible to various states of consciousness, a prerequisite to reality shifting.

Another psychological phenomenon that enables reality shifting is the natural ability to disconnect from certain thoughts and memories and link to others. This allows a person to detach from their present self and shift into a future or alternate version. By engaging in deliberate dissociation, you can become absorbed in alternate realities. Moreover, you lose awareness of your current surroundings, including the worries and limiting beliefs that may hinder you from achieving your goals. With safe practice, you won't lose your sense of self but gain awareness of another self that has achieved your desired outcomes. You also dissociate yourself from the limiting time of your current reality and breach the boundaries of other realities, where everything you dream of is possible.

Lastly, engaging your imagination further improves your ability to shift into any reality you want to explore. By learning how to conjure engaging and awareness-boosting mental images and scenarios, you're immersing yourself in the reality you want to manifest. More importantly, you can make emotional connections between your future or alternate self and your current self, creating empathy and motivation to work toward the goals you have achieved.

It's essential to approach reality shifting with openness. The technique allows you to explore your inner world and find desires and goals you want to align yourself with in other versions of yourself. Yet, simultaneously, it takes practice to safely shift from your current reality to whatever reality you wish to explore.

Consciousness in Quantum Theory

Quantum mechanics, a branch of quantum physics, states that to observe any matter, you must break it down to its simplest form: energy. Matter is seen as a unique version of energy, where movements happen through energy shifts.

According to a similar interpretation, quantum particles exist in multiple states (particle and wave) simultaneously. However, as particles shift from one state to another, scientists only see one state. At another time, the particles may shift to another state and can also be observed in that state. This phenomenon explains why particles give different results at diverse observational times. It all depends on which state is being observed. This is called the observer effect – the principle stating that changes in observation can change how the observed object behaves (or, more precisely, how the observer perceives it).

Consciousness also influences how people perceive something, especially if combined with the observer effect. Physicist Wolfgang Pauli – in collaboration with renowned psychiatrist Carl Jung – studied synchronicity (coincidences in which he believed he could affect the matter around him). He concluded that a person can influence their surroundings by thought. The founder of quantum physics, Max Planck, had similar beliefs, establishing the foundation for studying metaphysical occurrences. One of these occurrences, according to Planck, was that matter is directly derived from consciousness.

Other scientists and psychologists studying quantum mechanics and its relation to metaphysical occurrences have theorized that the way consciousness creates matter can also be tied to the law of attraction. This law states that what you focus on will come into your life because the thoughts you focus on in your consciousness are converted into energy. This energy attracts what you focus on. If you focus on positive thoughts, these will convert into positive energy, which attracts even more positivity. Conversely, if your consciousness is focused on negativity, your thoughts will become negative energy that draws negativity to your life.

Today, quantum physics widely accepts the belief that consciousness is a fundamental process in nature. All beings, including humans, are thought to be able to manipulate matter and energy around them.

Once again, drawing on Max Planck's teachings, it can be established that all matter exists because a force changes its energy or vibrations, as the energy phenomenon became known in popular nomenclature. This force is the power of the individual, which, in humans, is tied to consciousness.

So, how does this discovery in quantum physics and the observer effect tie into the practice of reality shifting? Consider this: If you have the power to manipulate your energy and the energy around you, you can change it to whatever form you want to see it. By altering your consciousness to focus on positivity, you can change the energies to positives – and attract these into your life.

Now, to the best part: You are the observer of energies. You see the energies around you change as you shift your consciousness. Once you start shifting your consciousness, what you see will change, too. You'll start seeing a new reality because you've changed how you observe yourself and the world around you. With practice, you can shift to any reality you wish by focusing your consciousness on it.

The Multiverse and Parallel Realities

The idea that there could be multiple versions of each individual is also tied to string theory, which implies that everything is composed of and held together by small strings. These string particles vibrate at different frequencies, making them unique parts of the individual and their environment. Moreover, these unique particles exist in several dimensions in space. You can see, observe, and experience only one dimension at a time, but there are many others where you and a version of your life exist. This opens up the implication of a multiverse, where the universe you live in is just one of the many that exist in a much larger whole. Each universe in this multiverse has its own laws where energy behaves differently – as do the particles that form people and their environment. In each, your energy and life differ from the one in your current universe. In some, the differences could be greater than you could ever imagine.

According to the multiverse theory, each universe is separated from the other by a membrane and exists in a higher dimensional space. There could be infinite universes, all divided by a membrane that can be crossed through reality shifting. You can visit each because they're a version of your reality. However, you must be aware of the possible changes in energies and vibrational frequencies when shifting to a new reality and version of yourself and your life. This is yet another powerful reason proper preparation and practice are fundamental for safe travel in the multiverse.

Still, if you feel at a crossroads and want to connect with another, more successful, and balanced version of yourself in another parallel universe, you can reach out and align yourself with their energy.

Aligning with a Desired Self

Now that you know that at least one of those realities and versions of yourself has achieved its goals, you may ask yourself, "How do I connect with them? How do I tune into what they're feeling, thinking, and experiencing?"

Visualization plays a massive role in identifying and connecting your successful self. To start visualizing this version of yourself, think about how it might differ from the current one. What does their life look like? What are some similarities between you? Finding something you have in common will make it easier to identify them.

Most people who ever imagine meeting their future self see themselves meeting a completely different person than they are now. However, this would mean you're trying to compare yourself with another person and not a version of yourself. No matter how many changes you implement, parts of you will always remain the same. You'll only be able to identify with a version of yourself if you can glimpse some similarities between you. So, rather than conjuring up an image of a stranger, visualize someone you can see yourself becoming. Alternatively, you can imagine meeting someone who lives the life you desire. The latter will prompt you to start making conscious choices to start living the life of the person you've visualized.

Unfortunately, along with imagining themselves as an action version of their person, most people also struggle with projecting their feelings and thoughts onto their future selves. After all, how would you know how your future self will feel about a positive outcome? If you're like most people, you'll either underestimate or overestimate the magnitude of your feelings in the future. For example, you might think that reaching a specific goal will bring you joy and happiness, and you won't be sad anymore. In reality, you'll still experience sadness because reaching one goal will not make other issues go away. This is another area where imagination will come in handy. You can imagine yourself realizing your goals despite all the hardships you might experience along the way.

By practicing visualization, you're divorcing yourself from the idea of seeing your future self as a stranger. The more you practice visualizing your successful future self, the more you'll believe you'll be that person one day. Moreover, the more connected you feel with your future self, the more motivated you'll be to work toward your goals and make those desired outcomes happen.

So, how do you align yourself with your future self's goals, aspirations, and actions? Here are a few tips:

- **Consider what your future self will value and enjoy.** By identifying values and likes you can relate to, you'll feel more empathetic toward your future self and start taking action to do what works for them. Don't just imagine what your future self has achieved. Think of what they would want to have. Otherwise, you won't be able to relate to them or care about their goals (consequently, you won't care about your goals either).

- **Visualize parts of your future selves live in tiny detail.** For example, instead of envisioning yourself living in your dream home, paint a picture of how this home will look on the inside. How will your future self-arrange their furniture? What art pieces will they appreciate in their home? Then, see your future self walk through the place as you go about your day.

- **Let the emotions come.** As you envision your desired self and outcome, you'll likely experience sudden feelings. Some of these may be negative. For example, you may feel afraid that you won't

be able to achieve the desired outcome. Acknowledge this. Intense emotions make the experiences (and the person experiencing them) more relatable.
- **Channel positivity.** When identifying and aligning with your future self, focus on the positive attributes. Show your future self that you have a positive view of them. If you see your future self capable of wonderful feats, it means you're capable of the same – and this positive vision may be why you start believing this.

Quantum Jump Meditation

By manifesting through a quantum jump meditation, you shift from your present reality into a reality where you've achieved the goal you're trying to manifest. The meditation below will help you access the parts of your mind capable of jumping and exploring new realities.

Instructions:
1. Get comfortable and set the intention to relax.
2. Take a few deep, relaxing breaths, enjoying the calm. The more mellow you get, the easier it will be to relax every fiber of your being.
3. Picture yourself on the beach. You're sitting cross-legged on the warm sand and hear the waves crashing at the shore near you.
4. The sun is shining on you, and you feel everything is perfect. Let yourself relax even more.
5. You dip your hand into the sand, and you can feel its texture in your hands. You look ahead and see the clear blue water meeting the beach's golden sand.
6. You're alone, and no one is there to disturb you.
7. Enjoy feeling relaxed and at ease. As you do, imagine yourself getting up and walking along the beach.
8. As you walk, feel the sand beneath your feet. You still hear the waves and birds flying by.
9. Suddenly, you come across a place where the ground splits and see steps leading down. Take them.
10. As you start going down, each step takes you deeper into relaxation, as if you're taking steps into yourself.

11. Notice how easy it is to relax, finding it naturally and breathing with a relaxed rhythm.
12. As you reach the final step, you notice that you've come far from the beach and are now entering darkness.
13. Even though it's dark, it feels good. Notice a small light in front of you. Walk toward it.
14. Now, you notice a pair of golden gates in front of you. Walk toward them, open them, and walk through them.
15. Suddenly, you find yourself in a vibrant place, with birds chirping and everything looking like a dream and not a reality.
16. Ask yourself what your dream is. What would you like it to look like if this was your dream reality?
17. As soon as you start describing your dream, notice how it starts to show up. For example, if you're dreaming about a new job, you're suddenly doing it in this dream reality.
18. As you experience it, consider how it makes you feel. How does it feel to achieve everything you want?
19. Think about how your life would be if you achieved everything. What would you do? Who would be with you? What would you do with them?
20. Enjoy being the person having these experiences. Think about one goal leading you to one of the experiences you enjoyed.
21. Then, imagine yourself achieving that goal. Congratulations, you've just quantum jumped into a reality where you can see yourself reaching your dreams and goals.
22. How do you feel now? Let everything else dissolve so that in this new reality, there is only you.
23. Think about creating the blueprint for making your desired reality come to life. See yourself going to the steps. How would you do it? What steps would you take?
24. With a new blueprint/intention in mind, slowly return to your present reality. Take a deep breath, wiggle your toes, and prepare to work toward your desired outcome.

Future Self Journaling

Have trouble imagining that your future self has reached all their goals? Write to them in a journal. You can write a letter or just a few random thoughts describing how your future self feels, what insights they've gained, and how they experienced the reality in which they've achieved all their goals.

Consider what you know now and the goals you set for yourself. Imagine what your future self will do differently from your present self. Then, tell yourself that you appreciate what they've achieved and want to know how they did it.

As you continue your letter or journal entry, visualize yourself doing something that reflects that you've achieved the desired outcome. Then, see your future self doing something you found useful for realizing your goals. Perhaps you've picked up a new habit or learned a new skill.

Make sure you pay attention to the emotions that pop up as you visualize your future self and are writing the lines to them. Contemplating what your future self is doing, is there anything you can hear, feel, smell, see, or taste that stands out? This will get your creativity flowing and motivate you to work toward the goals your future self has already achieved. It'll also help you set more specific intentions to manifest these goals.

Writing to your future self about your shared goals reinforces your intent to achieve them. You're planting them deep into your subconscious to remain rooted even if you face challenging situations, empowering your intentions even more.

Set a time to write to yourself regularly. Take 30-60 minutes to sit in silence and without disruption and contemplate what you want to say to your future self. Use your favorite writing tools (you can even use different colored ink if this helps enhance your creativity).

Another tip is to write as if you were writing to a friend, describing your achievements. After all, your future self will be just as happy about these achievements because they're theirs, too – just like a good friend would when hearing about your successes.

Determine a precise time and moment of your future life and write to yourself as if everything happened exactly how you wanted it to by this moment. Even as you do this, you may be inspired by new ideas for achieving your goals. If this happens, write these in a separate entry after you write your letter.

As always, use positive, kind language, and don't remind your future self of anything negative. You want to write about what you want to happen – to attract and manifest it. You don't want anything negative to happen, so you shouldn't write about it either.

Don't worry whether everything you write about your future self will be true. Some things may not, and you may experience some pleasant and some not-so-pleasant surprises. The goal is to encourage yourself to manifest and work toward your goals by showing how successful you can be in an alternate future reality.

The Mirror Technique

Mirror exercises are perfect for rehearsing many aspects of spiritual practices, including talking to your future self and seeing just how successful you can be. This exercise is similar to the one from the affirmations chapter, except here, you'll be talking to your future self – the self that has achieved all the goals you set for yourself.

Instructions:
1. Sit or stand in front of a mirror.
2. Visualize your future self looking back on you from the mirror. Create as detailed an image as possible by envisioning how you'll look, what you'll wear, etc.
3. Look deeply into the eyes of your future self and greet them.
4. Tell yourself how great you look and how happy you are focusing on yourself. Congratulations on achieving all your goals and not letting anyone snatch away your dreams.
5. Look at your future self and see how different you are. See how much you've achieved and how hard you've worked to become who you wanted to be.
6. Your future self may tell or show you that although you doubted yourself, you still did it. You were open to new possibilities and used these to lead you toward your goals.
7. Tell your future self about all the goals you've reached. Whether it's a dream job, continuing your education, eliminating toxic people from your life, inviting loving and caring individuals, or anything else, acknowledge that your future self has accomplished this and that you know it.

8. Tell your future self that you are especially proud that they didn't give up when it was hard initially. Eventually, everything will fall into place, and there will be no more insurmountable obstacles on your path.
9. Your future self has everything you want. Let the mirror image motivate you to work toward your goals. Life may throw you a curveball or two before you get there, but you know you'll be able to dodge them and keep thriving. You know this because you saw your future self's confidence and fulfillment when you looked into their eyes.
10. Before you let the image of your future self in the mirror go, tell them that if you ever start questioning yourself, remember your goals and why you set them. Reinforce how proud you are of your future self and tell them you can't wait to walk in their shoes one day.

Shifting with Intention

Proper preparation is crucial for successful quantum jumps, and part of the prep process is setting clear and specific intentions. How do you do this? You start by cultivating the right mindset, beginning with letting go of limiting beliefs and distractions. Consider what helps you focus and what doesn't. By practicing the first and stopping the second, you can formulate and set the right intention for manifesting your goals and dreams after shifting realities without getting sidetracked.

Preparing your mind for intention setting also means opening it for the process. Instead of letting doubt or judgment hinder your intention-setting practice, trust that you'll be able to set the right one. When you learn to set clear intentions, you can elevate your manifestation practice to a whole new level. You'll be opening the gate to a world of new possibilities – the only catch is that you must be open to explore them.

Your intention will help you achieve whatever goal you set for yourself in your quantum jumping practice, but it's also fundamental for safe travel. It takes you to whichever reality you want to explore, as long as you clearly state it in the first place. So, take as much time as necessary to ponder what you desire and where you want to go. Identify a specific goal, write it down, and read it out loud. How does it feel? Does it feel right, like it is what you're meant to do? If it does, you've found the perfect intention and can channel it before your next quantum jump.

Want to learn another trick to set clear intentions and reinforce them? Try visualization. You might need to train your imagination a little to conjure vivid images of the reality you want to manifest, but the result will be worth it. Close your eyes before you start, and take a few relaxing breaths before every visualization attempt. Try to bring up the desired reality, starting with sample images. Do this every morning after waking up and every evening before going to bed. Once you master these images and use them successfully to reinforce your intentions before jumping, move on to more complex scenarios and practice those.

Chapter 8: Daily Manifestation Rituals and Routines

Like any other practice, manifestation works best when incorporated into a regular schedule. This chapter offers morning and evening manifestation rituals you can integrate into your daily and weekly routines and helpful tips on making manifestation a regular part of your life.

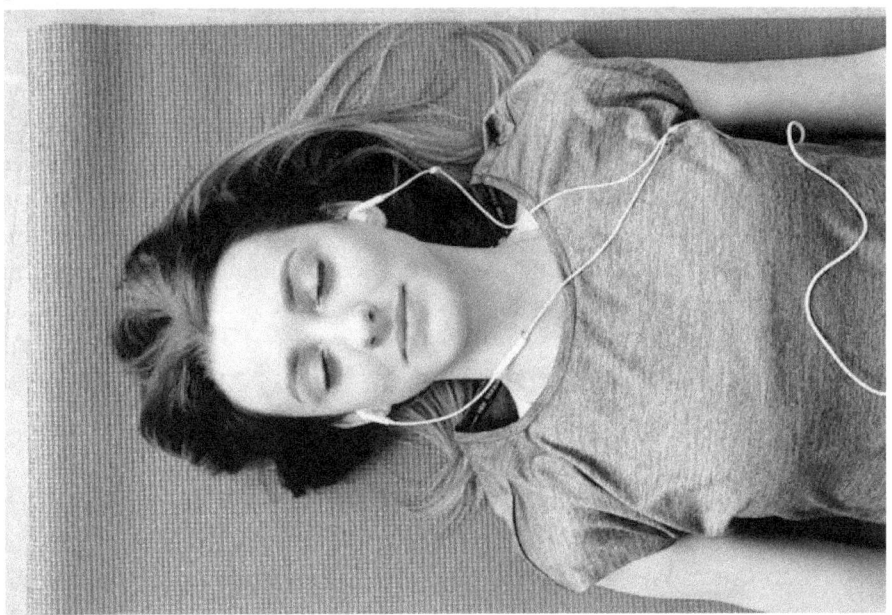

Manifestation works best when incorporated into a regular schedule.[86]

The Role of Routine in Manifestation

Manifestation requires the act of focused intention repeatedly. Consistency is key for strengthening the connection between your desires and goals and their realization. You can't rely on sporadic manifestation efforts if you want to transform your life through effective goal-setting and realization. Why? As you well know, manifestation works through energy channeling. You'll have a much higher chance of reaching your goals by directing your energy toward consistently realizing them.

When you incorporate a practice into your daily routine, you won't have to spend as much time with it. With simple, small steps, manifestation can become as natural as daily chores you've been doing for years, and you'll only have to spend a few minutes every day to achieve this.

Both routines and manifestation have something in common – they work best when tailored to your needs and preferences. By integrating your manifestation into a routine that works for you, you're creating time and space for yourself to work on whatever's important for you. The steps and routine should be something you can realistically do, even on busy days. While it's recommended to start and end your day with a manifestation practice and fit in some minutes in between, too, you should commit to this if you truly think you can. As you'll see shortly below, none of these have to be elaborate practices (although you can make them longer if you wish and have time for it). Even 10 minutes of getting up earlier to do a quick visualization or write a few lines in your journal and reinforce your manifestation with a 10-minute gratitude practice before bedtime can do the trick. The goal is to devise a frame for your consciousness, where you integrate all the positive thoughts and intentions you use to manifest your goals and dreams.

Morning Intentions to Set the Day's Energy

Mornings can be busy, but tuning your mindset toward your manifestation from the start of the day makes you more receptive to opportunities that align with your goals and desires. If you feel you can't spend much time with a manifestation practice after waking up, set your alarm 30 minutes earlier than usual. You'll have more time to evoke a morning intention.

Then, when you wake up and become fully conscious, do a quick, 10-minute meditation affirming your goals. You can combine this with visualization and do a 20-minute meditative visualization, where you close your eyes and imagine yourself achieving your goals. Alternatively, instead of meditation/visualization, you can repeat several positive affirmations after a quick meditative moment when you wake up. To do this, sit up in bed, take a deep breath, and repeat affirmations that align with your goals. It will help you start every day in harmony with what you want to manifest and achieve.

Ending the Day with Gratitude

It's no secret that realizing how many things you can be grateful for can improve your mood. Instead of focusing only on what you don't have or can't do, practicing gratitude teaches you how much you have and can do. This is particularly crucial when trying to manifest your goals. Appreciating the progress you make along the way is a massive confidence booster and a great way to reinforce a positive mindset.

Practicing gratitude boosts vibrational energy, making it fundamental for using the law of attraction to your advantage. Regularly focusing on what you feel thankful for will raise your vibrations, and your mind will project positive energy. Remember, you need positive thoughts and emotions to attract positive outcomes, and feeling grateful will give you exactly that.

By focusing on what you have instead of what you lack, you can shift your perspective to a more positive one. Just as a morning manifestation ritual opens you to new opportunities, so does an evening gratitude practice. Practicing gratitude can enhance your creativity, which you can use to manifest new opportunities, abundance, and success. It can also motivate you to work more diligently toward the goals you're trying to manifest.

Instead of focusing on feeling grateful for the obvious (for example, having positive, inspiring, and helpful individuals in your life, opportunities to grow, or material goods), consider showing appreciation for everything else that contributes to your success. The adversities you face aren't just there to hinder you. They're learning opportunities waiting to be explored and used. So, when they arise, express your gratitude toward them, too, as they'll help you learn how to problem solve and thrive.

Don't use words like but and if when practicing gratitude in the evening. Don't say, "I'm grateful for ... today, but if I could ... tomorrow, it will be much better." Also, only use gratitude statements that express what you're genuinely thankful for. If you don't truly feel grateful for anything, don't say it because it won't come from your heart or help you attract positivity.

To start an evening gratitude practice, set a time for it in the evening (around 30 minutes before going to bed). If you want to write down what you appreciate, take a pen, a piece of paper, or a journal and set it on the bedside table. Go through everything and everyone in your life to see what you feel grateful for. Practice this general appreciation first, and then, you can move on to more goal-specific gratitude statements. Consider the goal and look at what you've achieved already. What steps did you take? What opportunities did you have to work toward the desired outcome? What did you learn from these opportunities?

Reinforcement Through Small Actions

Try integrating other practices between your morning and evening rituals to reinforce your manifestation throughout the day. By taking just a few minutes a day to continue channeling your intentions, you will keep your mind focused on your goals and align with your desires.

These don't have to be monumental actions. It can be as simple as quickly visualizing your goal at the right time. For example, if you want to manifest a better job position, imagine yourself at your new workplace every time you complete a work task at your current job or when you do something to obtain a new job (learn a new skill, improve the old one, take action to educate and prove yourself, etc.).

Likewise, suppose your goal is to heal or improve your life. In that case, you can do a quick mental affirmation to reinforce the positive energy you're trying to attract to realize your goal. Affirmative statements reassuring you that you're healing or have healed (present-tense statements are incredibly powerful in the future) or have improved will help you raise your vibrations and manifest your intentions.

Whatever your goals, what matters is that the small actions you take toward them are consistent. You must repeat them regularly, at least two to three times a week.

Sample Manifestation Routine

Want to know the easiest way to use the law of attraction to manifest your desires? Create a complete manifestation routine. Here are two sample suggestions: one daily and one weekly.

Daily manifestation routine:

1. Start your day with hydration. It gives your metabolism and mindset a boost.
2. Write in your manifestation journal. You can script or record the lessons learned throughout the practice or whatever you want.
3. Clean your space to make room for abundance.
4. As you head toward midday, look at your vision board.
5. Around midday, light a candle or a focus-enhancing incense.
6. Work on raising your vibrations in the afternoon. Listen to meditation sounds or music to raise your vibrations.
7. Practice gratitude in the evening.
8. Let go of negativity and wait for positivity to join you as you prepare to end the day.

Weekly manifestation routine sample:

1. **Monday: Focus on Relaxation** - Start your week with relaxing exercises that help you let go of negativity and focus on positivity. These can include gratitude practices to acknowledge any negativity in your life and/or meditation to embrace your thoughts and feelings before letting them go.

   Once you have acknowledged the negativity, *channel some compassion and kindness toward yourself.*

2. **Tuesday: Enhancing Your Intuition and Creativity** - Now that you've cleared your mind yesterday, you continue relaxing and feeling grateful for everything you can and can do today. After practicing gratitude, bring your awareness to what you want to manifest. If you don't know what it is yet, try visualizing something that aligns with your goals. If you know what you want to manifest, continue your day with visualization and meditative exercises to enhance your focus on the desired outcome. As you do these, continue breathing deeply and relaxing. Depending on whether you've just started your manifestation journey or are already on

your way today, you may also want to look out for signs that what you're manifesting is becoming a reality. Focus on getting in touch with your intuition to encounter the signs in your daily life. If you notice any, take a mental note of them, then record them in your journal in the evening.

3. **Wednesday: Expressing Yourself** – After focusing on what you want to manifest and perhaps identifying signs of progress, turn to kindness and appreciation again today. Practice meditation and deep breathing exercises that help you relax and channel self-compassion. Once you have created a more positive mindset through gratitude, reinforce what you want to manifest by reciting it aloud or in your mind's eye.

4. **Thursday: Finding Emotional Balance and Empowerment** – Today, you concentrate on reinforcing your intention through positive affirmations. It's the ultimate day for balancing out the negativity and positivity and devising a positive mindset. You have channeled the desired outcome and made a connection with it, and now you should repeat it as if it has already happened. Besides affirmative practices, express your appreciation again for what you'll receive as if you've already obtained it. Have a little more time on this day? Incorporate some intuition-enhancing exercises like meditation, journaling, or visualization, too.

5. **Friday: Boosting Your Willpower** – Start with a relaxation practice and techniques focusing on what you want to manifest. Once again, affirm your outcome as if you've already realized it. Afterward, incorporate techniques to concentrate your energy and its power. For example, you could do a visualization exercise in which you imagine your energy outward from your body and feel it empowering your will and intention. Taking in the empowering sensation today will liberate you from any remaining hindering negativity.

6. **Saturday: Empowering Your Imagination** – Start the day with a practice that channels compassion and gratitude. Reinforce your intention to manifest the desired outcome with positive affirmation practices. Then, bring your awareness to your empowering energy and the progress you've already made toward your goal. You can do visualization to bring your awareness and the desired outcome to focus as if it has already happened. Notice your feelings and thoughts at the end of the day.

7. **Sunday: Completing The Manifestation** - Today, you complete the weekly manifestation process, fully reinforcing the mindset and energy to provide you with the desired outcome. You're bringing positive thoughts, goals, and steps needed to realize them into your consciousness. Repeat all the steps you've completed during the week in today's practices. Channel compassion, acceptance, and gratitude, repeat what you want to manifest and affirm it as it has already happened, embrace the positive emotions and your energy, and visualize how your life will be once you've realized your goals. You don't have to spend the full day doing this. Now that you've already spent the week taking them, five minutes with each step will be enough to fully reinforce your manifestation.

Morning Intention-Setting Ritual

Intention setting can be as engrossing or simplistic as you want it to be. In the morning, perhaps a short technique works best. Here is a simple morning practice: Set an intention for the day, visualize achieving it, and say affirmations. It won't take much time but sets the tone for a productive day.

Instructions:
1. As soon as you wake up, sit or stand comfortably. If you've opened your eyes, close them again.
2. Breathe deeply through your nose and out your mouth, relaxing your shoulders. With each inhale, try to take in a little more air into your lungs, allowing your chest and belly to expand.
3. Soften your jaw and eyelids. After your next inhale, hold your breath for 3 seconds.
4. Imagine your breath flowing in and out of you - as if it were water emanating from its source. Allow it to cleanse your system.
5. Continue breathing as you start focusing on your intention. Nothing else is in your awareness. Just the intent to manifest your goals.
6. As you take your next inhale, visualize yourself achieving your ultimate goal.
7. Take an even bigger breath, soften your body, relax your muscles, and repeat your affirmations.

8. Repeat the previous steps three more times, feeling your intention in your body, knowing it will come to reality.
9. Quickly express your appreciation for the outcome you'll receive as if you've already obtained it.
10. Let your intention infuse your energy. When you're ready, slowly open your eyes. You'll be ready to start the day while your intention works for you, helping you make conscious choices throughout the day toward your goal.

This morning's intention setting works best if you create one intention at a time. Your focus is the strongest in the morning, so use this to your advantage and empower one intention with it. Even if you set many goals, you'll be more likely to realize them if you don't try to channel several intentions simultaneously.

Evening Gratitude Practice

Just like a simple gratitude practice will set the tone in the morning, a brief, reflective exercise in the evening will allow you to review your day and reflect on and express your appreciation for your progress, no matter how small.

Remembering that you have so many little things to be thankful for just before sleep helps your mind focus on the positive experiences even as it processes the day's events and stores them in your subconscious. It will help you sleep better because you won't be distracted by negativity and overly wound up processing information at the end of the day.

Instructions:
1. At bedtime, sit down in a quiet corner and go over your day from when you got up in the morning until you sat down just now.
2. Can you name something you feel grateful for on this day? (Remember to enlist the negative experiences, too!) Avoid generalization, and be specific when considering everything you appreciate.
3. When considering the negatives, consider how you could turn them into positives. For example, if you feel that you couldn't complete something because you needed to help someone, consider what you gained. You had more time to spend with this person. Perhaps you grew your bond with them so they would become a stronger ally in reaching your goals.

4. Now, consider how many things you feel grateful for are connected to your goals.
5. If you have more than 10 minutes to spend on this gratitude exercise, write what you appreciate on this day in your journal. If not, say them out loud before taking a deep breath and releasing your gratitude into the air. Alternatively, you can record it on your phone and listen to it when you need a reminder of how far you've come in manifesting your goals.
6. Repeat this exercise every night for two weeks. Then, see if you find more things to be grateful for and if you have more appreciation for your progress.

Scripting Journal Routine

Writing about your ideal day (for example, a day in your life from a time when you've achieved your goals) as if you're already living it will reinforce your manifestation and desire every day.

Reinforce your manifestation and desire every day.[87]

Instructions:

1. Start in the morning as soon as you wake up. Open up your journal and try to answer the following and similar questions. How would your day look if you woke up on the day you've achieved your goal? What does lying in the bed feel like? Is it quiet around

you, or do you hear the noise of the bustling city? What time is it? Look around your bedroom. Is there any detail you can pick up that will tell you about your success? Describe everything in as much detail as possible, and, as always, use the present tense and the first person. However, don't overthink what you're going to write. Just write what comes to mind when answering these questions and describing your ideal day.

2. What do you feel after waking up? What emotions do you carry with you? Are you happy? Do you feel fulfilled? Where do these emotions come from? Do they come from reaching your goal or from what reaching this goal represents to you?

3. Do you do any exercise in the morning? What do you wear? What does the furniture around you look like?

4. If your perfect day includes working at a new position, describe how you go to work, what you wear, who you meet first when you get to work, etc. Describe your workplace in just as much detail as you did your home and bedroom. This applies to any other goal - when it involves an activity in a specific place, describe it and the place in detail.

5. Have fun writing about the different parts of your day. Then, set it aside. You can revisit it later when you're closer to manifesting your goals. You'll gain clarity about where you're headed and the motivation to work toward it.

Visualization Breaks

As eager as you are to manifest your desires or to advance toward your goals, trying to work without breaks will likely hinder your focus rather than empower it. Don't see breaks as a waste of time. Instead, try to view them as opportunities to relax and do a quick visualization. You're reigniting your focus when you take a mental break from everything around you. Do you know why? Your brain is constantly working. While concentrating on working toward your goals, your brain is busy maintaining your focus. It doesn't have time to process and recall memories, activate imagination, or other cognitive functions. By taking a break from focus and doing a quick visualization, you're helping your brain access all its other functions. In turn, you may have new insights or ideas, something you lacked while being overly focused.

Taking mental breaks will also prevent burnout and fatigue and keep your cognitive functions and energy on point. You'll have more (positive) energy to channel toward your intention to manifest your desires.

The best part? You decide when to take a break. However, it is recommended that you take at least a 30-minute break after several hours of hard work (even if it is working toward a goal). Whenever you feel overwhelmed by tasks, worries, or feelings about your ability to reach your goal or how to do it, take a short break to visualize your goal. Visualizing your goal will boost your motivation far more than working relentlessly.

Affirmation Reminders

Affirmations can be challenging to incorporate into a busy schedule. Fortunately, there are countless ways to remind yourself to practice affirmation and keep your mindset channeled toward goal manifestation. With these reminders, you won't have to worry about forgetting to recite affirmations or slacking off while trying to keep your vibrations high and positive.

Nowadays, affirmation reminder apps can be lifesavers. They will remind you to recite your preset affirmation statements at regular intervals. You can either write them down in the app or keep your affirmation cards with you at all times so you can read them whenever the reminder goes off.

Always maintain a positive attitude toward the task and yourself when using affirmation reminders. A reminder going off or affirmations displayed in your app might seem inconvenient on a busy day, but that's why you set them in the first place - to remind you of your goals when you're too busy to do it yourself.

Some apps will offer to write the affirmations for you. Whether you opt for this or write them yourself, ensure they're in the present tense and the first person. Alternatively, if you have only one or two affirmations, you can set them up as a screensaver on your phone, computer, or tablet.

Some may find using apps too impersonal because they lack emotional charge. If you feel this way, record yourself saying the statements in a compassionate but convincing voice. It's guaranteed to reach your heart. Hearing how much you want it and believe in it will make you work even harder toward the goal.

Alternatively, you can also place visual reminders, like sticky notes or vision birds, in a place you frequent regularly, such as your home, workplace, or wherever you want to reach that dream outcome. Write your affirmations in these places or use them as simple reminders to recite them to ensure you won't lose sight of your goal.

Whether you use apps, physical reminders, or any other reminder tool, use them at least once a day to keep them (and your attention) charged with your energy and desire to reach your goals.

Conclusion

As you reach the end of this journey, it's time to reflect on all the knowledge you gained from this book. It's time to put the skills you've developed into practice and put this new-found power to the test. You now understand how to use the art of manifestation to transform your life and bring your deepest desires to life. Whether you're new to the practice or more seasoned, the exercises and techniques provided in this book will help you succeed in this endeavor.

This book helped you understand the connection humans have with the world around them and delved into how your thoughts, intentions, and the universe are interconnected. You should now realize that the words you speak into the universe and the energy you exude to it are potent enough to come to life.

In the previous chapters, you learned about the theory behind manifestation. Also, you learned how to use methods like 369 and quantum jumping to create a life that aligns with your dreams. However, for these techniques to work, you must always keep in mind that your flexibility, ability to embrace change, willingness to take leaps of faith, consistency, and determination are essential.

You should also avoid thinking of manifestation as a destination. It should be an ongoing practice, even if your deepest desire becomes a reality. Manifestation is about enhancing your life and taking control of it. It involves cultivating energies of gratitude, abundance, and opportunities all day, every day. Incorporating the strategies and routines suggested in this book into your daily life can help you establish a positive mindset and attract endless opportunities. You will find that all you need and more are flooding into your life.

The journey of manifestation and developing the skills you need to bring your dreams to life will help you point you toward personal growth and development. You become cognizant of the fact that you're the creator of your reality and that your thoughts and feelings can shape your reality. This is why you must always be mindful of your desires, intentions, and thoughts.

It won't always be easy to stay in the energy and mindset of gratitude and abundance, especially when life becomes testing. You now possess the tools to overcome and rise above these challenges. You can return your focus to your goals and reclaim your power by practicing visualization, journaling, and saying positive affirmations. This will reaffirm your confidence, release self-doubts, and remind you of your ability to manifest your dreams.

Good luck, and may all your dreams come true!

If you enjoyed this book, I'd greatly appreciate a review on Amazon because it helps me to create more books that people want. It would mean a lot to hear from you.

To leave a review:
1. Open your camera app.
2. Point your mobile device at the QR code.
3. The review page will appear in your web browser.

Thanks for your support!

Here's another book by Mari Silva that you might like

Your Free Gift
(only available for a limited time)

Thanks for getting this book! If you want to learn more about various spirituality topics, then join Mari Silva's community and get a free guided meditation MP3 for awakening your third eye. This guided meditation mp3 is designed to open and strengthen ones third eye so you can experience a higher state of consciousness. Simply visit the link below the image to get started.

https://spiritualityspot.com/meditation

Or, Scan the QR code!

References

Part 1: Spirit Messages

8 Types Of Spirit Guides & How To Communicate With Them. (2023). Tony Womersley. https://www.tonywomersley.com/blogs/8-types-of-spirit-guides-how-to-communicate-with-them/

A Complete Guide to Psychic Protection and Psychic Self-Defense. (2024, April 18). https://www.psychicsource.com/article/other-psychic-topics/a-complete-guide-to-psychic-protection-and-psychic-self-defense/24918

Alan. (2022, February 14). The 7 Different Types Of Spirit Guides - Subconscious Servant. Subconscious Servant - Mindfulness, Spirituality & Self-Care. https://subconsciousservant.com/types-of-spirit-guides/

Allen, S. (2024, May 12). A Guide to Mediumship Symbols and Signs . Susan Allen Medium. https://susanallenmedium.com/a-guide-to-mediumship-symbols-and-signs/

Anima Mundi Herbals. (2021, May 11). What are Spirit Guides? And How Do You Communicate with Them? Anima Mundi Herbals. https://animamundiherbals.com/blogs/blog/what-are-spirit-guides-and-how-do-you-communicate-with-them

Animal Guides, Totems, Symbolism, Messengers and Meaning. (2015, September). Beautifulgroovyawesomegreat. https://beautifulgroovyawesomegreat.com/2015/09/01/animal-guides-totems-symbolism-messengers-and-meaning/

Aura Health Team. (2023). White Light Meditation: Embrace Purity and Clarity with White Light Meditation. Aura. https://www.aurahealth.io/blog/white-light-meditation

Bartlett, J. (2018, April 6). Symbols as Messages from Spirit, Your Loved Ones and Your Inner Self. Jeaux Bartlett. https://www.alightintuition.com/intuition/the-signs-and-symbols-you-get-from-spirit/

Beckler, M. (2016, January 16). Angel Numbers – Learn the Angel Number Meanings Today. Ask-Angels.com. https://www.ask-angels.com/spiritual-guidance/angels-and-numbers/

Beckler, M. (2016, September 23). Who Is Your Guardian Angel? And How Can You Connect With Them? Ask-Angels.com. https://www.ask-angels.com/spiritual-guidance/who-is-your-guardian-angel/

Beckler, M. (2019, December 2). Angel Signs ~ 13 Signs Your Angels Are With You! Ask-Angels.com. https://www.ask-angels.com/spiritual-guidance/angel-signs/

Beckler, M. (2020, July 5). 7 Types of Spirit Guides - Which Are On Your Spiritual Team? Ask-Angels.com. https://www.ask-angels.com/spiritual-guidance/types-of-spirit-guides/

Bell, A. (2017, April 15). 9 Most Common Signs of Communication from Spirit | Angie Bell Spiritual Medium. Angie Bell Spiritual Medium | Spiritual Guidance. https://angiebell.com/9-most-common-signs-of-communication-from-spirit/

Belsito, T. (2017, August 17). 12 Common Signs Spirits Send Us to Let Us Know They Are Around! Medium. https://medium.com/@tonybelsito/12-common-signs-spirits-send-us-to-let-us-know-they-are-around-98890b34db87

Carter-King, B. (2018, December 4). What is a Spirit Animal | Spirit Animal vs Totem Animal vs Power Animal. What Is My Spirit Animal. https://whatismyspiritanimal.com/what-is-a-spirit-animal-and-whats-the-difference-between-a-spirit-animal-vs-totem-vs-power-animal/

Desirée. (2023, May 8). The Difference Between Animal Spirits, Guides + Totems. Mojave + Wolf. https://www.mojaveandwolf.com/the-blog/difference-between-animal-guides-spirits-and-totems

Detchon, A. (2018, June 11). The Importance of Grounding and Protecting Your Energy. Linkedin.com. https://www.linkedin.com/pulse/importance-grounding-protecting-your-energy-andrea-detchon-bsc-

Drake, M. (2019). Journey To Meet Your Power Animal. Blogspot.com. https://shamanicdrumming.blogspot.com/2019/11/journey-to-meet-your-power-animal.html?utm_source=chatgpt.com

Embracing Shamanism. (2023, August 15). How Does Shamanism Relate to Nature and Ecology? Embracing Shamanism. https://www.embracingshamanism.org/2023/08/how-does-shamanism-relate-to-nature-and-ecology/

Ferreira, D. (2024, October 5). Angel Messages: How to Receive Them and What They Mean. AskAstrology. https://askastrology.com/life/angel-messages-how-to-receive-them-and-what-they-mean/

Franklin, S. (2023, November 17). The 4 Clairs and How They Are Used in an Intuitive Reading. Intuitive Coaching. https://www.samintuitivecoach.com/post/the-4-clairs

Fraser, M. (2022, February 18). The Most Common Signs From Spirit. Meet Matt Fraser. https://meetmattfraser.com/the-most-common-signs-from-spirit/

Gaia Staff. (2014). 3 Spirit Animal Meditations: Contact Your Animal Guide | Gaia. Gaia. https://www.gaia.com/article/3-spirit-animal-meditations

Greenlaw, F. (2018, December 28). What are Spirit Guides? 5 Things Everybody Gets Wrong. The Wellness Foundry. https://wellnessfoundry.co.uk/what-are-spirit-guides/

Jordan. (2024, September 11). Spirited Earthling. Spirited Earthling. https://www.spiritedearthling.com/mindfulness-and-meditation/helpful-basic-spiritual-protection-practices-you-need-to-know

Journey, T. E. (2024, April 27). Animal Spirit Guides: Finding Your Totem Animal. The Enlightenment Journey. https://theenlightenmentjourney.com/animal-spirit-guides-finding-your-totem-animal/

Kaiser, S. (2022, March 30). 4 Exercises to Build Trust and Confidence in... | Spirituality+Health. Spirituality+Health. https://www.spiritualityhealth.com/4-exercises-to-build-trust-and-confidence-in-your-intuition?utm_source=chatgpt.com

Keen Editorial Staff. (2016). Psychic Advice and Meditation Aid Connection With Spirit Animals - Keen Articles. Keen.com. https://www.keen.com/articles/psychic/psychic-advice-and-meditation-aid-connection-with-spirit-animals

Kleiman, D. (2024, September 19). Myths Busted: The Truth About Spirit Guides No One Tells You - Dina Kleiman - Energy Healer, Intuitive Reader, Spiritual Teacher. Dina Kleiman - Energy Healer, Intuitive Reader, Spiritual Teacher. https://dinakleiman.com/myths-busted-the-truth-about-spirit-guides-no-one-tells-you/

Kulick, D. (2021, August 12). Angels, Spirit Guides, Ancestors: Are Souls of the Dead Watching over Us? | Something to Think About. Pocono Record. https://www.poconorecord.com/story/lifestyle/columns/2021/08/12/angels-spirit-guides-ancestors-souls-dead-watching-us/5556392001/

Lather, K. (2022, April 26). Spirit Guides & Guardian Angels. Angel Connections. https://www.angelconnections.com.au/blog/spirit-guides-amp-guardian-angels

ledbysource. (2019, September 8). Third Eye Visualization. Ledbysource. https://ledbysource.com/third-eye-visualization/

Linette, A. (2014, September 9). Light Spirits: What's The Difference Between Guardian Angels & Spirit Guides? Amanda Linette Meder. https://www.amandalinettemeder.com/blog/2014/9/9/light-spirits-what-is-the-difference-between-guardian-angels-and-spirit-guides

Mills, A. (2024, September 11). Common Signs & Symbols From Loved Ones In Spirit. Arlene Mills. https://arlenemills.com/common-signs-symbols-from-loved-ones-in-spirit/

Monahan, J. B. (2018, June 18). Spiritual Messages and Experiences – Getting, Interpreting and Encouraging More. Medium. https://medium.com/@jennifermonahan_28426/spiritual-messages-and-experiences-getting-interpreting-and-encouraging-more-6fa2b8332d99

Mysticsense. (2020, June 24). What Are Angel Cards and How to Use Them | Mysticsense. Mysticsense. https://www.mysticsense.com/articles/oracle-cards/angel-cards-and-how-to-use-them/

Nicholson, S. (2014). 10 Signs That Spirit Is Trying to Communicate with You. Suenicholson.co.nz. https://www.suenicholson.co.nz/blog/10-signs-that-spirit-is-trying-to-communicate-with-you/

North, S. (2023, September 30). Demystifying Spirit Guides: The Truth About Their Role and Origins. Medium; Heart Speak. https://medium.com/heart-speak/demystifying-spirit-guides-the-truth-about-their-role-and-origins-e69392394858

Pavlina, E. (2011, August 4). What are the Four Clairs of Psychic Ability? • Erin Pavlina, Intuitive Counselor. Erin Pavlina, Intuitive Counselor. https://www.erinpavlina.com/blog/2011/08/what-are-the-four-clairs-of-psychic-ability/

Pearce, J. (2020, March 9). 5 Ways To Connect With Your Guardian Angels. Mindbodygreen.com. https://www.mindbodygreen.com/articles/ways-to-connect-with-guardian-angels

Pearce, K. (2023, April 18). 10 Mindful Walking And Nature Connection Practices. Mindful Ecotourism. https://www.mindfulecotourism.com/the-art-of-mindful-walking-meditation-practices/

Rankin, L. (2015, March 4). 18 Ways To Strengthen Your Intuition. Mindbodygreen. https://www.mindbodygreen.com/articles/how-to-strengthen-your-intuition

Reality Pathing. (2025). 3 Simple Chakrubs Techniques for Daily Energy Alignment | Reality Pathing. Realitypathing.com. https://realitypathing.com/3-simple-chakrubs-techniques-for-daily-energy-alignment/

Redford, N. (2024, October 18). Animal Spirit Oracle Cards: Unlocking Intuition and Emotional Guidance for Personal Growth. The Indie Spiritualist. https://theindiespiritualist.com/animal-spirit-oracle-cards/

Reiss, A. (2023, March 24). 4 Types of Spirits That Departed Loved Ones Become | California Psychics. California Psychics. https://www.californiapsychics.com/blog/psychic-tools-abilities/medium/spirits-departed-loved-ones-become.html

Richardson, T. C. (2017, June 13). How To Use Your Intuition Like A Professional Psychic. Mindbodygreen. https://www.mindbodygreen.com/articles/the-4-types-of-intuition-and-how-to-tap-into-each

Romano, A. (2024, January 30). Master Simple Techniques for Manifestation and Energy Alignment. Affirm Your Reality. https://affirmyourreality.com/simple-techniques-for-energy-alignment-in-manifestation/

Runa Heilung. (2024, January 8). Journey to Meet Your Spirit Animal - Old Soul Alchemy - Medium. Medium; Old Soul Alchemy. https://medium.com/old-soul-alchemy/journey-to-meet-your-spirit-animal-70d57455984e

Samford, L. (2022, June 14). Walking Nature Meditation for Deeper Connection. Lena Samford. https://lenasamford.com/walking-nature-meditation-for-deeper-connection/

Sara. (2024). Connect With Your Spirit Guide, Meditation Script. Letsmovemindfully.com. https://letsmovemindfully.com/meet-your-spirit-guide/

Sayce, A. (2021, June). Can Deceased Loved Ones Become Our Spirit Guides After They Pass? Anna Sayce. https://annasayce.com/can-deceased-loved-ones-become-our-spirit-guides-after-they-pass/

Signs from the Universe. (2025, January 18). How to Identify Your Nature Spirit Guide. Signsfromtheuniverse.guide. https://signsfromtheuniverse.guide/how-to-identify-your-nature-spirit-guide/

Snyder, K. (2022, January 25). Looking for Stronger Intuition? Try This Third Eye Meditation. Yoga Journal. https://www.yogajournal.com/meditation/third-eye-meditation-for-intuition/

Sun. (2024, May 19). Rooted Sun. Rooted Sun. https://www.rootedsun.co/blog/11-simple-exercises-to-unlock-your-third-eye

The Enlightenment Journey. (2023, June 18). Psychic Self-Defense: Techniques and Strategies - The Enlightenment Journey - Medium. Medium; Medium. https://medium.com/@tej88/psychic-self-defense-techniques-and-strategies-d62fcee2eff4

The Enlightenment Journey. (2024, August 17). How to Use Meditation and Visualization with Ascended Masters. The Enlightenment Journey.

https://theenlightenmentjourney.com/how-to-use-meditation-and-visualization-with-ascended-masters/

The Enlightenment Journey. (2024, May 15). Types Of Spirit Guides: Finding Your Spiritual Allies. The Enlightenment Journey. https://theenlightenmentjourney.com/types-of-spirit-guides-finding-your-spiritual-allies/

The Enlightenment Journey. (2024, October 5). Connecting with Your Guardian Angel. The Enlightenment Journey. https://theenlightenmentjourney.com/connecting-with-your-guardian-angel/

The Enlightenment Journey. (2024a, April 27). Fairy Spirit Guides: Communicating with Nature's Spirits. The Enlightenment Journey. https://theenlightenmentjourney.com/fairy-spirit-guides-communicating-with-natures-spirits/

The Enlightenment Journey. (2024b, April 27). Nature Spirit Guides: Channeling Earthly Energies. The Enlightenment Journey. https://theenlightenmentjourney.com/nature-spirit-guides-channeling-earthly-energies/

The Enlightenment Journey. (2024c, June 6). Elemental Spirits: Earth, Air, Fire, Water. The Enlightenment Journey. https://theenlightenmentjourney.com/elemental-spirits-earth-air-fire-water/

The Reforest Nation Team. (2023, February 5). Nature & Folklore: An Interwoven Legacy in Ireland. Reforest Nation. https://www.reforestnation.ie/blog/nature-folklore-an-interwoven-legacy-in-ireland

Tully, S. (2023, January 24). How To Connect To Spirit Guides – Sonia. Soniatully.com. https://soniatully.com/2023/01/24/how-to-connect-to-spirit-guides/

Webster, R. (2022, June 13). 7 Ways to Connect with Archangels. Llewellyn Worldwide, Ltd. https://www.llewellyn.com/journal/article/3023

Wicked Obscura. (2024, August 29). Signs That Your Spirit Guides Are Trying to Communicate with You. Wicked Obscura Apothecary. https://www.wickedobscura.com/blog/2024/8/29/signs-that-your-spirit-guides-are-trying-to-communicate-with-you

Wolf, M. (2022, March 27). 6 - The Intuitive Nudge - Path of Courage. Path of Courage. https://pathofcourage.com/the-intuitive-nudge/

Your Higher Journey. (2021, February 15). What Are Ascended Masters? This Guide Explains All Your Higher Journey. https://www.yourhigherjourney.com/numerology/what-are-ascended-masters/

Part 2: Manifestation

13 Common Limiting Beliefs Holding Us Back. (2023). Career Contessa. https://www.careercontessa.com/advice/limiting-beliefs/#examples

5 Best frequency for manifestation. (2024, October 23). Mahakatha.com. https://mahakatha.com/blog/best-frequency-for-manifestation/#439ae22cd46442279f2f22eaf0be9537

6 Steps to Breaking Your Limiting Beliefs. (n.d.). PushFar. https://www.pushfar.com/article/6-steps-to-breaking-your-limiting-beliefs/

Abbadia, J. (2024, May 13). Infinite Possibilities: Understanding The Multiverse Hypothesis. Mind the Graph Blog. https://mindthegraph.com/blog/multiverse-hypothesis/

Aby. (2014, January 10). How to Create a Vision Board. Simplify 101. https://simplify101.com/organizing-blog/create-vision-board/

Admin. (2018, May 31). *Why You Should Use An Affirmation Reminder App.* ThinkUp App. https://thinkup.me/affirmation-reminder/

Bamber, R. (2024, October). THE POWER OF VISUALISATION: A BRAIN-FRIENDLY TOOL FOR GOAL ACHIEVEMENT AND LEADERSHIP. Rachel Bamber. https://www.rachelbamber.com/the-power-of-visualisation-a-brain-friendly-tool-for-goal-achievement-and-leadership/

Bean, L. M. (2017, November 8). *LinkedIn.* Linkedin.com. https://www.linkedin.com/pulse/quantum-leaping-change-your-life-jump-lisa-bean/

Biddulph, R. (2015, May 6). Law of Attraction: Moving into Alignment and Staying There (As Much as Can!) Part 1 – Home. Livelifemadetoorder.com. https://www.livelifemadetoorder.com/blog/law-of-attraction-alignment-part-1/

Bloom, C., & Bloom, L. (2019, September 12). Self-Trust and How to Build It | Psychology Today. Www.psychologytoday.com. https://www.psychologytoday.com/intl/blog/stronger-the-broken-places/201909/self-trust-and-how-build-it

Bonnard, P. (2024, March 14). 60 Limiting Beliefs Examples | Thoughts That Hold You Back. Starchaser-Healing Arts. https://www.starchaser-healingarts.com/60-limiting-beliefs-examples-thoughts-that-hold-you-back/

Borowski, S. (2012, July 16). *Quantum mechanics and the consciousness connection | American Association for the Advancement of Science (AAAS).* Www.aaas.org. https://www.aaas.org/taxonomy/term/10/quantum-mechanics-and-consciousness-connection

braceybee. (2018, October 31). Braceybee. https://www.braceybee.com/blog/law-of-attraction-alignment-before-action

Bradberry, M. (2020, February 6). Living Better Lives Counseling LLC. Living Better Lives Counseling LLC. https://www.livingbetterlivesnwa.com/blog/2020/1/25/diy-affirmation-cards-and-how-to-use-them

Brennan, D. (2021, April 12). What Are Binaural Beats? WebMD. https://www.webmd.com/balance/what-are-binaural-beats

Brown, B. (2021, September 20). Law of Vibration | The 12 Universal Laws of Manifestation. Modern Manifestation. https://www.themodernmanifestation.com/post/law-of-vibration

Capritto, A. (2024, November 17). The Best Meditation Apps for Reducing Stress in 2024. CNET. https://www.cnet.com/health/sleep/best-meditation-apps/#google_vignette

Charlie. (2020, January 29). *Consider writing yourself a letter from the future - www.yourtimetogrow.com*. Www.yourtimetogrow.com. https://yourtimetogrow.com/writing-a-letter-from-the-future/

Cherry, K. (2022, October 6). 10 Ways to build resilience. Verywell Mind. https://www.verywellmind.com/ways-to-become-more-resilient-2795063

Cherry, K. (n.d.). How to Use a Vision Board to Achieve Your Goals. Verywell Mind. https://www.verywellmind.com/how-to-use-a-vision-board-to-achieve-your-goals-7480412#toc-how-to-make-your-own-vision-board

Chuney, A. (2024). *LinkedIn*. Linkedin.com. https://www.linkedin.com/pulse/harmonic-numerology-unlocking-sacred-vibrations-numbers-andrez-chuney-ckx5c/

Cirino, E. (2018, July 19). 6 Ways to Build Trust in Yourself. Healthline. https://www.healthline.com/health/trusting-yourself#bottom-line

Clark, J. (2023, September 6). Does a Parallel Universe Really Exist? HowStuffWorks. https://science.howstuffworks.com/science-vs-myth/everyday-myths/parallel-universe.htm#pt1

Cohen, Y. (2024, November 14). Top 10 Best Meditation Apps in {year}. Www.top10.com; Top10.com. https://www.top10.com/best-lists/best-meditation-apps

Connor-Savarda, B.-N. (2023, April 1). The Science Behind Emotional Energy: Exploring the Vibrations of Our Emotional World | Emotional Intelligence Magazine. EI Magazine. https://www.ei-magazine.com/post/the-science-behind-emotional-energy-exploring-the-vibrations-of-our-emotional-world

Davis, T. (2020). What Is Manifestation? Science-Based Ways to Manifest. Psychology Today. https://www.psychologytoday.com/intl/blog/click-here-for-happiness/202009/what-is-manifestation-science-based-ways-to-manifest

Deniz, F., Nunez-Elizalde, A. O., Huth, A. G., & Gallant, J. L. (2019). The Representation of Semantic Information Across Human Cerebral Cortex During Listening Versus Reading Is Invariant to Stimulus Modality. Journal of Neuroscience, 39(39), 7722–7736. https://doi.org/10.1523/JNEUROSCI.0675-19.2019

Des Marais, S. (2013, October 17). *5 Ways to Trust Yourself More*. Psych Central. https://psychcentral.com/relationships/how-to-develop-self-trust#alone-time

Doty, J. R. (2024, May 7). *What We Get Wrong About Manifesting*. TIME; Time. https://time.com/6975041/manifesting-science-essay/

Dr.Nile. (2024, August 16). *How To Do Quantum Jumping? Meaning and Methods - Goddess*. Goddess Wellbeing for Women. https://www.goddesswomenapp.com/blog/how-to-do-quantum-jumping/#cultivating-the-right-mindset

Ducksters. (2018). *Science for Kids: Crystals*. Ducksters.com. https://www.ducksters.com/science/crystals.php

Eatough, E. (2023, February 22). *What Is The Law Of Attraction And Can You Use It To Change Your Life?* Www.betterup.com. https://www.betterup.com/blog/what-is-law-of-attraction

Eyal, N. (2022, September 29). *The Surprising Science of "Manifestation."* Nir and Far. https://www.nirandfar.com/science-of-manifestation/

Garaca Djurdjevic, M. (2023, March 6). *ifa*. Ifa.com.au. https://www.ifa.com.au/opinion/32484-the-top-10-self-limiting-beliefs-and-how-to-let-them-go

Goldman, R. (2024, November 19). *Affirmations: What They Are and How to Use Them*. EverydayHealth.com. https://www.everydayhealth.com/emotional-health/what-are-affirmations/#sample-affirmations

Gottlieb, L. (n.d.). *What About the Quantum Physics Observer Effect?* Larry Gottlieb Author. https://www.larrygottlieb.com/blog/the-observer-effect

Graham, A. (2024, September 16). *Transform Your Life with the 55x5 Manifestation Method*. Simplyashleygraham.com. https://simplyashleygraham.com/transform-your-life-with-the-55x5-manifestation-method/

Gupta, S. (2023, November 9). *Sound Healing for Self-Care*. Verywell Mind. https://www.verywellmind.com/sound-healing-for-self-care-8384146

Gupta, S. (2024, September 23). *How to Manifest Your Goals With the 369 Method*. Verywell Mind. https://www.verywellmind.com/manifest-your-goals-with-the-369-method-8620625

Guveya, N. (2023, May 31). *The Benefits of the 9 Solfeggio Frequencies*. The Pulse Blog. https://ouraring.com/blog/the-benefits-of-the-9-solfeggio-frequencies/?srsltid=AfmBOopbjFW-xj3KaNXwJRbG2oT6bKefrW0e5F4blbgAnxo1JSU3bLLg

Hart, A. (2024). *How To Create A Beautiful Oracle Deck In 8 Steps*. The Occult Witch. https://theoccultwitch.com/blog/2018/4/17/how-to-create-a-beautiful-oracle-deck-in-8-steps

Hartoonian, Dr. N. (2020, January 6). The Power of Visualization: Imagining Yourself Doing Something Helps You Achieve Your Goal. Rowan Center for Behavioral Medicine. https://www.rowancenterla.com/the-power-of-visualization-imagining-yourself-doing-something-helps-you-achieve-your-goal/

Helmenstine, A. M. (2019). What Is a Crystal? ThoughtCo. https://www.thoughtco.com/what-is-a-crystal-607656

Hermetic Chaos. (2023, June 20). Unlocking Your Potential: The Powerful Five-Step Manifestation Formula. Medium. https://medium.com/@hermeticchaos777/unlocking-your-potential-the-powerful-five-step-manifestation-formula-eb19dd0bfdb5

How can you make your visualizations more vivid and engaging with sensory details? (2023). Linkedin.com. https://www.linkedin.com/advice/0/how-can-you-make-your-visualizations-more

How to be more patient: 7 ways to cultivate patience. (2023, October 18). Calm Blog. https://www.calm.com/blog/how-to-cultivate-patience-in-your-daily-life

Howell, E. (2018, May 10). Parallel Universes: Theories & Evidence. Space.com; Space.com. https://www.space.com/32728-parallel-universes.html

HowStuffWorks. (2024, October). Unlocking the Power of 3, 6, and 9: Exploring the 369 Manifestation Method. HowStuffWorks. https://science.howstuffworks.com/science-vs-myth/extrasensory-perceptions/369-method.htm#pt2

HowStuffWorks. (2024, October). *Unlocking the Power of 3, 6, and 9: Exploring the 369 Manifestation Method.* HowStuffWorks. https://science.howstuffworks.com/science-vs-myth/extrasensory-perceptions/369-method.htm

Insight Network, Inc. (2024). Insight Timer - #1 Free Meditation App for Sleep, Relax & More. Insighttimer.com. https://insighttimer.com/amandasellers/guided-meditations/manifest-an-abundant-life

Insight Network, Inc. (2024). *Insight Timer - #1 Free Meditation App for Sleep, Relax & More.* Insighttimer.com. https://insighttimer.com/danikadoucet/guided-meditations/morning-ritual-intention-setting-breathwork

Jarvis, C. (2024, May 8). Stanford Neurosurgeon on the Science of Manifestation | Chase Jarvis. Chase Jarvis Blog. https://chasejarvis.com/blog/stanford-neurosurgeon-on-the-science-of-manifestation/

Jean, Erin. (2024). *Quantum Jumping Meditation.* Insighttimer.com. https://insighttimer.com/erinjean/guided-meditations/quantum-jumping-meditation

Jewell, A. (2020, November 11). *Amanda Jewell.* Amanda Jewell. https://theamandajewell.com/blog/manifestation-routine

Justin. (2023, July 24). Here's How I Created an Affirmation Card Deck from Scratch: My Step-by-Step Process - SoCurious. SoCurious. https://socurious.co/heres-how-i-created-an-affirmation-card-deck-from-scratch-my-step-by-step-process/

Kalia, A. (2022, February 3). *"My life completely turned around": is manifesting the key to happiness – or wishful thinking?* The Guardian. https://www.theguardian.com/lifeandstyle/2022/feb/03/my-life-completely-turned-around-is-manifesting-the-key-to-happiness-or-wishful-thinking

Karpaski, D. (2024). LinkedIn. Linkedin.com. https://www.linkedin.com/pulse/easily-achieve-your-goals-mental-movie-method-karpaski-m-a-nbcch/

Kavi B. (2023, July 19). Quantum Entanglement and Parallel Realities: Investigating the Relationship between Entanglement and the Existence of Parallel Worlds. Medium. https://medium.com/@iamkavib/quantum-entanglement-and-parallel-realities-investigating-the-relationship-between-entanglement-379e048524e3

Kehoe, J. (2022, December 26). Are Thoughts Energy? How to Use Them to Influence Reality. Mind Power. https://www.learnmindpower.com/are-thoughts-energy/

King, J. (2015, December 28). Janelle King. Janelle King. https://www.janelleaking.com/blog/mindset-manifestation

Koosis, L. (2024, September 26). *The Science Of Affirmations: The Brain's Response To Positive Thinking*. MentalHealth.com. https://www.mentalhealth.com/tools/science-of-affirmations

Learn the science behind visualization and how it works. (n.d.). EnVision. https://envision.app/visualization/the-science-of-visualization/

LinkedIn Community. (2023, December 6). *Learn how taking breaks can enhance your creativity, productivity, and well-being, and how to plan and take effective breaks for your creative problem-solving.* Linkedin.com. https://www.linkedin.com/advice/0/how-can-taking-breaks-improve-your-creative-speue

Lover, L. (2021, July 13). *Using The Scripting Manifestation Technique To Attract Anything You Want.* One Latte Too Many. https://onelattetoomany.com/using-the-scripting-manifestation-technique-to-attract-anything-you-want/

Makabee, H. (2023, October 30). Replacing Limiting Beliefs with Empowering Beliefs. Effective Software Design. https://effectivesoftwaredesign.com/2023/10/30/replacing-limiting-beliefs-with-empowering-beliefs/

Malu, N. (2022, January 5). It's all about vibrations, man! A theory in which I do believe for life. Our comprehension of the world is not solely about what we glimpse, vocalize, listen to and cogitate. Linkedin.com. https://www.linkedin.com/pulse/vibing-frequency-life-neha-malu-/

Maria. (2024, August 29). Reviewing the Top 9 Affirmation Apps. Vision Board ++. https://www.thevisionboard.app/top-affirmation-apps-iphone/

Mayo Clinic Staff. (2020, October 27). How to Build Resiliency. Mayo Clinic. https://www.mayoclinic.org/tests-procedures/resilience-training/in-depth/resilience/art-20046311

Mayo Clinic. (2023, December 14). Meditation: A simple, fast way to reduce stress. Mayo Clinic. https://www.mayoclinic.org/tests-procedures/meditation/in-depth/meditation/art-20045858

MBA, C. M., Psychologist. (2019, March 4). *Positive Daily Affirmations: Is There Science Behind It?* PositivePsychology.com. https://positivepsychology.com/daily-affirmations/#science

McCormick, A., & Owens, H. (2024, January 31). These 7 Apps Will Deepen Your Meditation Practice. Verywell Mind. https://www.verywellmind.com/best-meditation-apps-4767322

McNally, M. (2024, May 1). *You Are Your Future Self: Learn How to Tune into Who You Want to Be.* Linkedin.com. https://www.linkedin.com/pulse/you-your-future-self-learn-how-tune-who-want-melanie-mcnally-psyd-b6hgc/

Meditation Benefits: Improve your Exercise Goals | Physique 57. (2021, January 5). Physique 57. https://physique57.com/meditation-can-improve-your-fitness-goals-heres-how/

Merritt, R. A. (2024, April 19). Visualization and manifestation have gained significant attention in recent years as powerful tools for personal growth, achieving goals, and creating the life we desire. While techniques and practices vary, there's one crucial element that serves as the explosive force behind these practices: emoti. Linkedin.com. https://www.linkedin.com/pulse/emotion-tnt-visualization-manifestation-raymond-merritt-8nmze/

Michael, E. (2024, September 26). The Science Of Manifestation: The Power Of Positive Thinking - MentalHealth.com. MentalHealth.com. https://www.mentalhealth.com/tools/science-of-manifestation

Mindom. (2024, April 9). Visualization is often viewed as a simple and perhaps even frivolous practice... Linkedin.com. https://www.linkedin.com/pulse/neuroscience-behind-visualization-effect-brain-our-emotions-nmkvf/

Minuto, A. (2024, October 17). The Process of Processing Emotions To Manifest - True Self Manifestation. True Self Manifestation. https://trueselfmanifestation.com/processing-emotions-to-manifest/

Modern Recovery Editorial Team. (n.d.). Visualization: Definition, Benefits & Techniques. Modern Recovery Services. https://modernrecoveryservices.com/wellness/coping/skills/cognitive/visualization/

Morreale, M. (2024, December 1). Manifestation Methods: Can You Really Get Everything You Want? Www.betterup.com. https://www.betterup.com/blog/manifestation-methods

Morreale, M. (2024, December 1). *Manifestation Methods: Can You Really Get Everything You Want?* Www.betterup.com. https://www.betterup.com/blog/manifestation-methods

Mosunmola, Z. (2023, January 24). *The String Theory and The Multiverse.* Medium. https://zainabmosunmola.medium.com/string-theory-and-the-multiverse-e31ecceba1495

Neil, S. (2024, August 26). *The Role of Gratitude in Manifestation | Mindset Motive.* Mindset Motive. https://mindsetmotive.com/role-gratitude-manifestation/

Ningthoujam, N. (2024, March 13). *Can the 369 manifestation method make your dreams come true?* Healthshots. https://www.healthshots.com/mind/mental-health/369-manifestation-method/

Novak, J. M. (2024, January 7). 62 Self-Limiting Beliefs that Block Happiness and Success • Believe and Create. Believe and Create. https://believeandcreate.com/62-beliefs-that-limit-your-happiness-and-success/

oneuponedown. (n.d.). Manifestation definition and how to practice it. OneUpOneDown - Women Mentoring. https://oneuponedown.org/blog-post/manifestation-definition-and-how-to-practice-it/

Pavel, I. (2023, June 16). *Simplish.* Simplish. https://simplish.co/blog/types-of-affirmations#affirmations-for-success

Perry, E. (2022, May 25). What Is a Manifestation Journal? A 9-Step Guide to Write Your Dreams. Www.betterup.com. https://www.betterup.com/blog/what-is-a-manifestation-journal

Perry, E. (2023, June 15). 5 steps to create a vision board that does its job. BetterUp. https://www.betterup.com/blog/how-to-create-vision-board

PHR, C. W. (2023, December 18). 🌌 Welcome to a realm where the laws of physics and the art of manifesting merge in an intriguing dance. In the world of quantum manifestation, we step into a reality where our thoughts, intentions, and desires are entangled in a mysterious web of interconnected possibilities. Linkedin.com. https://www.linkedin.com/pulse/unlocking-mysteries-manifesting-quantum-physics-depth-colin-w-jjxhc/

Porat, A. (2021, July 19). LinkedIn. Linkedin.com. https://www.linkedin.com/pulse/how-harness-power-your-focused-intention-amazing-now-ada-porat-ph-d-/

Primed Mind. (2021, September 26). 14 Benefits of Guided Meditation Backed by Science. Primed Mind: The Best Mindset & Hypnosis App. https://primedmind.com/benefits-of-guided-meditation/

PURI, M., & ROBINSON, D. (2007). Optimism and Economic Choice. Journal of Financial Economics, 86(1), 71–99. https://doi.org/10.1016/j.jfineco.2006.09.003

Ravindran, D. (2024, June 3). The Power of Manifesting: Turning Thoughts into Reality. Medium. https://deepakravindran.medium.com/the-power-of-manifesting-turning-thoughts-into-reality-d6ce5a03e898

Ries, J. (2024, October 9). I'm a Neuroscientist. Here's Why I Believe in the Power of Manifestation. SELF. https://www.self.com/story/neuroscientist-science-behind-manifestation

Rivendell Marketing. (2022, April 19). A Guide to Crystal Grids for Beginners. Rivendell Shop. https://rivendellshop.co.nz/blogs/default-blog/a-guide-to-crystal-grid-for-beginners

Rogers, D. (2024, June 25). Have you ever felt out of sync with yourself, where your emotions, thoughts, and actions seem to pull you in different directions? Linkedin.com. https://www.linkedin.com/pulse/power-alignment-dave-rogers-hzttc/

Romano, A. (2024, January 30). Unlock Your Desires: A Guide to Energy Alignment & Manifestation. Affirm Your Reality. https://affirmyourreality.com/what-is-the-science-of-energy-alignment-and-manifestation/

Ross, M. (2024, July 9). What Is Manifestation, and Does It Actually Work? We Asked Mental Health Experts. @Onepeloton; Peloton Interactive. https://www.onepeloton.com/blog/what-is-manifesting/

Ryan, T. (2021, June 22). Binaural Beats for Sleep. Sleep Foundation. https://www.sleepfoundation.org/noise-and-sleep/binaural-beats

S., K. (2023, May 16). LinkedIn. Linkedin.com. https://www.linkedin.com/pulse/understanding-law-vibration-how-your-thoughts-affect-life-selvakumar/

Samayla Jewellery. (2024, August 13). Manifesting with Crystals: A Guide to Attracting Your Desires. Samayla Jewellery. https://www.samayla.co.uk/blogs/samayla-blog/manifesting-with-crystals-a-guide-to-attracting-your-desires

Saxton-Thompson, C. (2020, April 22). *Evening Gratitude Practice - Wholehearted Life Therapy | North Palm Beach, FL.* Wholehearted Life Therapy | North Palm Beach, FL. https://wholeheartedlifefl.com/blog/evening-gratitude-practice/

Scott, A. (2015, March 11). The Power of - The 2X CEO - Medium. Medium: The 2X CEO. https://medium.com/the-2x-ceo/the-power-of-focused-intent-96d59ddfc4f5

Scott, E. (2020, November 18). Understanding and using the law of attraction in your life. Verywell Mind. https://www.verywellmind.com/understanding-and-using-the-law-of-attraction-3144808

Scripting for Manifestation: A Step-by-Step Guide - Centre of Excellence. (2024, February 8). Centreofexcellence.com. https://www.centreofexcellence.com/scripting-for-manifestation/

Scurio, J.-M. (2023, August 20). Thoughts, Emotions, and Intentions. Iloveureka! https://www.iloveureka.com/post/thoughts-emotions-and-intentions

Sesay, A. (2024, January 16). The Complete Guide to Oracle Cards. ELLE. https://www.elle.com/horoscopes/a46333458/best-oracle-card-decks-guide/

Sirivarangkun, W. (2020, August 16). 8 Best Meditation Apps of 2023 to Practise Calm and Focus. Mindful Wonderer. https://mindfulwonderer.com/best-meditation-apps/

Sneha. (2023, February 21). Mastering the Art of Reality Shifting: How to Use Parallel Realities for Manifestation. Medium. https://snehagm1207.medium.com/mastering-the-art-of-reality-shifting-how-to-use-parallel-realities-for-manifestation-%EF%B8%8F-f63fe478ef7f

Sood, P. S. (2021, July 6). *The 7 7-Day Meditative Manifestation Routine!* Linkedin.com. https://www.linkedin.com/pulse/7-day-meditative-manifestation-routine-parmeet-singh-sood/

Team Asana. (2021, November 29). 10 limiting beliefs and how to overcome them. Asana. https://asana.com/resources/limiting-beliefs

Tempera, J., & Talbert, S. (2022, March 27). *The 369 Manifestation Method Has Taken Over TikTok, And TBH, I Can See Why.* Women's Health. https://www.womenshealthmag.com/life/a39518396/369-manifestation-method/

Tewari, A. (2022, June 12). *How to Effectively Write Affirmations and Practice Them + Examples.* Gratitude - the Life Blog. https://blog.gratefulness.me/how-to-write-affirmations-how-to-do-affirmations/

Thalia. (2023, July 3). 17 Guided Journal Prompts for Goal Setting | Notes by Thalia. Https://Notesbythalia.com/. https://notesbythalia.com/journal-prompts-for-goal-setting-and-reviewing-progress/

The 12 Best Crystals for Manifesting Your Dreams - Centre of Excellence. (2024, January 12). Centreofexcellence.com. https://www.centreofexcellence.com/crystals-for-manifesting/

The Manifestation Collective. (2020, February 27). *How To Use Scripting To Manifest.* The Manifestation Collective. https://themanifestationcollective.co/scripting-to-manifest/

The Science of Manifestation: How Visualization Can Help You Create Your Own Reality. (2023, August 30). WindowStill. https://www.windowstill.com/the-science-of-manifestation-how-visualization-can-help-you-create-your-own-reality/posts/

The Secret Witch. (2024, June 14). The Power of Mindset in Manifesting: Why Actionable Steps are Key to Achieving Your Dreams. Medium. https://medium.com/@renatadaniel_60327/the-power-of-mindset-in-manifesting-why-actionable-steps-are-key-to-achieving-your-dreams-0bc3231c77ac

Travers, M. (2024, July 2). A Psychologist Explains The Phenomenon Of "Reality Shifting." *Forbes*. https://www.forbes.com/sites/traversmark/2024/03/20/a-psychologist-explains-the-phenomenon-of-reality-shifting/

Travers, M. (2024, March 29). A psychologist explains the power of "vision boarding" for success. Forbes. https://www.forbes.com/sites/traversmark/2024/03/29/a-psychologist-explains-the-power-of-vision-boarding-for-success/

True Vibes Unleashed. (2021, January 28). *True Vibes Unleashed*. True Vibes Unleashed. https://www.truevibesunleashed.com/pet-professional-blog/intention-setting

University of Miami. (n.d.). *Soothing Affirmations*. https://fsap.miami.edu/_assets/pdf/Flyers/affirmations-and-breathing-exercise-handout.pdf

Urezzio, Jennifer. (2020, January 24). *Your Personal Formula for Manifesting Your Vision - Kind Over Matter*. Kind over Matter. https://kindovermatter.com/your-personal-formula-for-manifesting-your-vision/

van Kempen, A. (2019a, January 5). The connection between Neuroplasticity and the Law of Attraction - Bujoo Academy. Bujoo Academy. https://bujooeducation.com/academy/is-there-a-connection-between-the-law-of-attraction-and-neuroplasticity/

Velez, H. (2023, January 13). What Is Manifestation? The Good Trade. https://www.thegoodtrade.com/features/what-is-manifestation-how-to/

Visualization meditation: 8 exercises to add to your practice. (2023, August 22). Calm Blog. https://www.calm.com/blog/visualization-meditation

Visualization to Calm Nervous System. (2023, September 23). Www.cibdol.com. https://www.cibdol.com/blog/1643-visualization-to-calm-nervous-system

Walker, T. A., & FSU Contributor. (2020, April 9). *Mirror, Mirror on The Wall: Hey Future Self*. Her Campus. https://www.hercampus.com/school/fsu/mirror-mirror-wall-hey-future-self/

Wander Art. (2023, August 2). 7 Steps to Personalized Positive Affirmations. *Wander + Art*. https://doi.org/1002956143/20230630_195254

Wellness design consultants. (2022, July). Wellness Design Consultants. https://biofilico.com/news/2022/6/22/sound-therapy-for-mental-wellbeing-the-top-5-apps-to-know

Willgress, L. (2024, November 28). Best mindfulness apps in 2024 to keep calm during a crisis. The Independent. https://www.independent.co.uk/health-and-fitness/best-mindfulness-apps-a8217931.html

Williamson, I. (2024, October 20). Tesla's Code to the Universe: Understanding the 369 Manifestation Method. Linkedin.com. https://www.linkedin.com/pulse/teslas-code-universe-understanding-369-manifestation-ipek-ev6rc/

Wooll, M. (2022, July 19). Don't let limiting beliefs hold you back. Learn to overcome yours. BetterUp. https://www.betterup.com/blog/what-are-limiting-beliefs

Zen, U. (2024). Insight Timer - #1 Free Meditation App for Sleep, Relax & More. Insighttimer.com. https://insighttimer.com/_ultimate_zen/guided-meditations/new-moon-meditation-solfeggio-frequencies-manifestation

Image Sources

1. Designed by Freepik. https://www.freepik.com/free-photo/numerology-concept-with-woman-posing_41252224.htm
2. https://www.pexels.com/photo/an-eagle-flying-in-the-sky-3250638/
3. https://www.pexels.com/photo/a-woman-engaged-in-fortune-telling-6944681/
4. https://www.pexels.com/photo/woman-sitting-on-brown-stone-near-green-leaf-trees-at-daytime-1234035/
5. Designed by Freepik. https://www.freepik.com/free-vector/body-chakras-concept_8515104.htm
6. https://www.pexels.com/photo/woman-closing-her-eyes-against-sun-light-standing-near-purple-petaled-flower-plant-321576/
7. https://www.freepik.com/free-photo/brown-eye-bright-background_31499094.htm
8. Designed by Freepik. https://www.freepik.com/free-psd/cartoon-angel-wings-isoltated_178832496.htm
9. https://www.pexels.com/photo/gray-feather-on-tree-stem-394376/
10. https://www.freepik.com/free-photo/overhead-view-eyes-closed-woman-lying-near-open-blank-book-blanket_5233812.htm
11. https://www.pexels.com/photo/white-and-black-wolf-397857/
12. https://www.pexels.com/photo/woman-in-black-top-sitting-on-brown-armchair-3331574/
13. Designed by Freepik. https://www.freepik.com/free-vector/animals-black-linocut-stencil-pattern-drawing-collection_16338492.htm
14. https://www.pexels.com/photo/worms-eyeview-of-green-trees-957024/
15. https://www.pexels.com/photo/woman-sleeping-935777/
16. https://www.pexels.com/photo/photo-of-person-standing-on-grass-2623878/
17. Designed by Freepik. https://www.freepik.com/free-photo/abstract-numerology-concept-with-man-seaside_36300065.htm
18. Designed by Freepik. https://www.freepik.com/free-vector/snihy-star-background_1177943.htm

19 https://www.pexels.com/photo/materials-for-witchcraft-and-burning-candles-on-a-round-table-7189446/

20 https://www.pexels.com/photo/close-up-shot-of-fortune-telling-objects-7221573/

21 https://www.pexels.com/photo/photo-of-person-holding-cup-3363111/

22 https://www.freepik.com/free-photo/young-girl-meditate-green-forest-with-sunlight_3952256.htm

23 https://www.pexels.com/photo/woman-meditating-with-candles-and-incense-3822864/

24 Photo by Lucas Pezeta: https://www.pexels.com/photo/woman-spreading-both-her-arms-2529375/

25 Original author unknow; colored by Ivar van Wooning, CC BY-SA 3.0 <https://creativecommons.org/licenses/by-sa/3.0>, via Wikimedia Commons https://commons.wikimedia.org/wiki/File:Nikola_Tesla_Colored.png

26 Photo by Binti Malu: https://www.pexels.com/photo/photo-of-a-sign-and-eyeglasses-on-table-1485657/

27 Photo by Matthias Cooper: https://www.pexels.com/photo/woman-in-green-shirt-smiling-1062280/

28 Photo by Mikhail Nilov: https://www.pexels.com/photo/person-woman-art-creative-6932015/

29 Photo by Photo By: Kaboompics.com: https://www.pexels.com/photo/photo-of-assorted-crsytals-4040639/

30 Photo by Antoni Shkraba Studio: https://www.pexels.com/photo/top-view-of-a-woman-in-getting-tibetan-singing-bowls-treatment-6252137/

31 Photo by Andrea Piacquadio: https://www.pexels.com/photo/content-woman-in-empty-hall-looking-out-window-4376623/

32 Photo by Polina   : https://www.pexels.com/photo/handwrting-letters-on-blue-sticky-notes-8709442/

33 Photo by Min An: https://www.pexels.com/photo/photo-of-man-looking-at-the-mirror-1134184/

34 Photo by Mikhail Nilov: https://www.pexels.com/photo/woman-in-red-dress-holding-fire-6931866/

35 Matthias Weinberger, Attribution-NonCommercial-NoDerivs 2.0 Generic CC BY-NC-ND 2.0 <https://creativecommons.org/licenses/by-nc-nd/2.0/deed.en> https://www.flickr.com/photos/51035610542@N01/58525360

36 Photo by Photo By: Kaboompics.com: https://www.pexels.com/photo/tranquil-woman-resting-on-yoga-mat-in-earphones-at-home-4498187/

37 Photo by Alina Vilchenko: https://www.pexels.com/photo/photo-of-person-holding-cup-3363111/

www.ingramcontent.com/pod-product-compliance
Lightning Source LLC
LaVergne TN
LVHW051916060526
838200LV00004B/164